ALFY'S
AMAZING BUT TRUE
TALES OF AMERICAN HISTORY & MORE

by
Alfred A. E. Wolfram

ALFY'S AMAZING BUT TRUE

TALES OF AMERICAN HISTORY & MORE

Andover,
Minnesota

ISBN 1-931945-21-7

Library of Congress Catalog Number: 2004110284

Printed in the United States of America

First Printing: September 2004

08 07 06 05 04   5 4 3 2 1

Andover,
Minnesota

Expert Publishing, Inc.
14314 Thrush Street NW,
Andover, MN 55304-3330
1-877-755-4966
www.expertpublishinginc.com

DEDICATION

The late Professor Henry Hull,
Professor of American history,
Winona State University.

He was a truly great teacher of American history,
an authentic one of a kind.

CONTENTS

CONTENTS

ACKNOWLEDGEMENTS

*W*hen approaching the completion of one's first book and looking back on all who have helped you throughout your life, it becomes a humbling experience, indeed. All of us are merely the composite of all of those who offered their shoulders for us to stand upon. They boosted us to a higher level of achievement than one could ever have imagined. My thanks include so many. Here are but a few:

- To an incredible wife and children, who have been ever supportive, always believing in my every adventure.

- My wonderful mother who sacrificed much.

- Mr. Stoltman, who taught me I could communicate.

- Mr. Stephans, who taught me a love for Shakespeare and how to write.

- My college freshman English professor who spurred me to succeed in writing when she told me, "Don't ever consider going into English; you haven't the mentality for it."

- Professor Henry Hull, who gave me a love for history and an insight into how to present it.

- All my many friends, especially Bob, Jerry, Ron, Oscar and Kevin, who have been there to love me, encourage me, and keep me focused.

- To my publisher, editor, book organizer, who helped so very much in making this book possible.

- To Bill Luse, one of the most talented illustrators in the nation.

- And finally, to you the reader, who has taken an interest in these, my many tales.

To all of you, I owe a heart-felt debt of gratitude.

INTRODUCTION

*H*istory is nothing more than lies agreed upon!" Those were the words Professor Henry Hull used to introduce me to my first college American history course. By the end of that first class period, however, he led me to understand that his statement was not exactly true. But Professor Hull's statement had garnered my attention.

In actuality, what a historian essentially does is gather facts, interpret those facts, and then edit those facts down to a presentational size, whatever that may be. It is during this most logical, time honored, process that some of the best stories of history are consigned to a dusty file drawer, only to be forgotten forever. It was Professor Hull who taught me that history, especially American history, is teeming with such stories, if one looks for them. These stories transcended even the most original and compelling fiction. And they were all true—for the most part.

As I continued to study history, I became puzzled by the Hollywood writers who departed from the historical truth, only to end up with a piece of fiction that not only clouded and confused history, but was often far less interesting and entertaining than the original historical facts. What writer of fiction has ever come up with tales to match Washington's false teeth helping to win a war, a pig determining the statehood of Texas, or a monument to a left leg?

The real history of this country does not consist of a few gigantic, though often dull, stories of mass migrations or colossal battles. The real history, the fun side of history, the meaningful side of history, has always been, and will always be, comprised of the activities of common people doing uncommon things.

Unfortunately, the truth of much of our history has often been deleted or ignored for one reason or another, usually determined by the politics of the time. When I was in high school, I read nothing of the contributions of the Buffalo Soldiers or few other African-Americans for that matter. All the cowboys in my childhood world were of European extraction, even though many historians now agree that upwards of one-third of all cowboys in the U.S. were African-Americans. Although I sought out information about every Caribbean pirate I could find, I saw no mention of women pirates. And I never remember being taught about a woman in the mid-1800s running for President or winning a Congressional Medal of Honor.

Fortunately, times are changing. Much of what is being taught in our history classes today has changed. When I taught my first class of American history in 1965 in Guthrie Center, Iowa, certain parts of what I presented in the classroom were considered very controversial and were challenged. Fortunately, I had a supportive administration and I prevailed. Today these same things are considered mainstream and almost passé. There is less of an effort to sanitize our history for the sake of trying to create a perfect image of our country. We are slowly beginning to realize that a country is like a person. To love it, truly love it, totally, unequivocally, one must know and accept its virtues as well as its flaws.

I have attempted to authenticate all the stories which you will read in this volume, separating fact from fiction, history from legend. If there are historical inaccuracies, we at Eirene Productions would like very much to receive supporting documentation.

I am certain that those "lies agreed upon," which we call history, will continue to evolve. But what will never change is the wonderfully rich abundance of stories to be found in our times of yore. Our past abounds with them. It was our ancestors, yours and mine, who lived what we now call history. With this in mind, we have established the "Tales of American History Preservation Society"(TAHPS). We are looking for those "amazing, but true" stories which may come from your ancestors or your family past for our next volume of *Alfy's Amazing But True…*

In the meantime, I hope you enjoy these first of *Alfy's Amazing But True Tales…* I truly feel that Professor Henry Hull would have loved them all. I hope you do!

A BUDGE AGAINST FACISM

*H*e would play what some described as the single most politically charged tennis match ever. Who was this tennis great?

Here are a few clues: member of the Tennis Hall of Fame, best all-time winning percentage for match play, best all-time doubles player, the only American to win the Grand Slam of tennis in the twentieth century, best all-time backhand. I am certain anyone who has ever picked up a racket will probably know that these credentials belong to none other than the great Don Budge.

Born in Oakland, California, in 1915, J. Donald Budge is considered by many experts to be the greatest tennis player of all times. His thunderous backhand, which consistently drove his opponent deep, was his calling card. Some feel we didn't see his equal until

Jimmy Connors came on the scene with his over-powering two-handed backhand, almost forty years later.

Because of a shoulder injury during World War II, many thought Budge's game was over. But his post-war victory over Poncho Gonzales proved to be one that Gonzales himself described as the most stinging defeat of his career.

Though Budge consorted with kings and queens, heads of state, and Hollywood movie stars, he led a very private life with his wife, Lori. In later years Budge became the elder statesman of tennis. When John McEnroe was fighting for the number one ranking, he turned to Budge for advice. Some say it changed McEnroe's game.

Budge believed a player had to undergo rigorous training, physically, technically, and mentally to reach one's best. He was said to be almost old fashioned in his insistence on courtesy and fair play.

But perhaps his 1937 Davis cup match against Germany's Baron Gottfried Von Cramm will be remembered the most by tennis fans. Von Cramm was the greatest German tennis player of his time. He and Budge were scheduled to meet for a pivotal Davis Cup match held at Wimbledon. As the two sat quietly together in the locker room, awaiting their match, the phone rang. It was none other than Adolph Hitler calling. The Fuhrer wanted to let Von Cramm know that, as a representative of the Master Race, all of Germany was counting on him to beat the American.

It was a tense moment. The eyes of the world were on this match. Who would come out the victor? Well—

Von Cramm started strong, as usual, winning the first two sets. But then, Budge came alive and powered his way back to capture the next two sets. The stage was set for one of the most dramatic final sets in the history of tennis.

Von Cramm brought forth every bit of skill he possessed and took the lead in the final set, four to one. But then, from some inner unknown reserve, Budge found unbridled courage and strength. With a backhand that was stronger than ever, he repeatedly drove Von Cramm deep. Finally, with the conviction of the true champion he was, Budge came back to defeat Von Cramm in that ultimate match, much to the dismay of Mr. Hitler.

Though he went on to many more great tennis victories, Don Budge will forever be remembered as the man who struck one of the first blows against Fascism—with a tennis racket.

A COUNTRY BUILT ON BIRD DROPPINGS?

*I*t's time for a little quiz on geography. Wait! Wait! Don't panic. This might be fun.

Question: "What is the smallest, and perhaps the richest, republic in the world?" Give up? The answer is Nauru. I know, I know, *where is Nauru?*

Nauru is a tiny little island republic northeast of Australia, nearly two hundred miles from its closest neighbor. Only eight square miles in size, its current population is just over 10,000, one third of whom are migrant workers. Nauru has no capital. All of its citizens live in rural areas.

Nauru was originally settled by Polynesian and Melanesian seafarers before any recorded history of this region. Eventually these inhabitants developed into twelve clans or tribes that trace their ancestral descent on the female side of the family. Having worshipped a female deity, Eijebong, for centuries, the local inhabitants led an isolated existence.

Unfortunately, the introduction of firearms and alcohol in the mid 1800s by whalers all but destroyed their peaceful co-existence and decimated almost half of their entire population.

Then in 1899, local farmers discovered that Nauru was almost entirely composed of phosphate, a prized fertilizer. It has been created by bird droppings and the remains of ancient sea creatures. This valuable nutrient quickly became its chief export. With its newfound prosperity, Nauru became ripe for exploitation.

After being pillaged by the Germans, British, Japanese, and Australians, the United Nations finally granted Nauru its independence from Australia in 1968. It was at this point the tiny state of Nauru took over ownership of the lucrative phosphate company. This has brought the people of Nauru unprecedented prosperity.

Today they pay no taxes and have outstanding health care for all their citizens, anywhere in the world. In addition, they are provided with free schools, telephone, and public transportation. Each local is given a home, rent free, with all bills and maintenance paid. Despite the fact there is only one paved road, about twelve miles long, many Nauruans own three or four cars.

But success hasn't totally changed this simple people. Most of the local citizens still sleep on mats, hand woven with their tribe's unique pattern. These patterns, along with tribal songs and stories, can't be used or copied by another tribe. One interesting custom is known as *Bubutsi*: if someone admires something of yours—a car, a boat, television, whatever—you immediately give it to them.

But is there darkness on the horizon for the people of Nauru? What will happen when the bird droppings are all gone? Will there be an end to this South Seas Shangri-La? Well—

Actually, the leaders of Nauru have been anticipating this for some time. Years ago they started investing large portions of their phosphate earnings for the future benefit of their people. At last tally, they owned a shipping line, airline, fishing corporation, five long-term trusts, hotels, and office buildings around the world, and the tallest skyscraper in Australia.

Although Nauru did experience over $8 million worth of losses due to fraud and mismanagement in the 1990s, they still have high hopes for the future. And who knows? Maybe someday you will have a vacation ticket stamped "Bound for Nauru."

A Lady Pirate?

*A*h, pirates! We all know what they looked like—a hulking man, with a patch over one eye, a hook for a hand, and a peg leg. But, did you know there were also women pirates? Oh yes, indeed! And perhaps, the most famous was a lass by the name of Anne Bonney.

The illegitimate daughter of an Irish lawyer, Bonney moved to the New World with her father in the early 1700s. A highly spirited woman, she married a sailor, against her father's wishes, in order to find excitement and adventure. Soon she became disillusioned with her husband's lazy, shiftless ways.

It was at this time Anne became smitten with a dashing sea captain, Calico Jack Rackham, with little regard for who in town knew it. Unfortunately the law of the time said that if a wife stepped out on her husband, she could be punished with a public flogging. Anne Bonney was so sentenced.

On the night before her public whipping was scheduled, she and Calico Jack slipped away, stole a sloop, and set out to sea. That was the start of their pirating career. The two plundered in a blissful union, as though they were made for each other and destined for a life of pirating.

Then one day, a new young sailor came aboard. Almost from the beginning Anne began spending a great deal of time with *him*. Finally, Calico Jack could stand it no longer. "I'll slit his throat!" he roared. As Jack reached for his dagger, the young sailor stopped Calico Jack in his tracks with a single action. What could he have done that would have stunned this enraged pirate so greatly? Well—

As Jack reached for his dagger, the sailor suddenly ripped open his own shirt and revealed to the captain that "he" was a "she".

That's right! The new crew member turned out to be a widow named Mary Reed. After the shock wore off, all became good friends. Mary Reed went on to wed a crewman, and they all continued in their pirating ways. And oh! If those two women didn't turn out to be the fiercest fighters you have ever seen. When attacking merchant ships, they could handle a broad sword with the best of them—until they discovered they were each pregnant.

So, the decision was made to set aside piracy and sail to Cuba, a haven for pirate families. But before they could reach Cuba, they were surprised by a British naval sloop, the *Curlew*.

Ann and Mary fought the British fiercely, while their men cowered below deck, with Calico Jack hiding in a clothes closet. Soon they were all captured, taken to Jamaica, convicted of piracy, and sentenced to be hanged. The night before the hanging, Calico Jack was visited by his beloved Anne, who said, "Because you couldn't fight like a man, you must die like a dog!" And with that she walked out of his life.

The two women avoided the hangman's rope because of their pregnancy. Mary eventually died in prison. But Anne Bonney was inexplicably released, and then just faded in history, apparently never to plunder again.

A MIGHTY SET OF TEETH

C an you imagine a set of false teeth affecting the outcome of a war? This very thing may have happened.

The year was 1781. George Washington was about to go into one of the largest and most important battles of the American Revolutionary War. He was about to engage none other than General Charles Cornwallis. The site of the battle was just outside of Yorktown, Virginia.

It was a critical time in the history of our newly declared nation. Washington needed every bit of concentration he could muster. But he had a real problem. It seems as though Washington was the proud possessor of a complete set of false teeth, upper and lower. They were made from elk's teeth that had been filed down and imbedded in a lead alloy. As one might imagine, these teeth were very heavy and uncomfortable. Often he would have to file them down himself. If they would break, he would have to send them back to his dentist in Philadelphia for repair or adjustment.

It was May of 1781. Washington was making plans to attack Cornwallis. Then, at a most inconvenient time, he started having a bit of a problem with his teeth.

So he sent a letter to his dentist, a Dr. Baker. Washington asked in the letter for two things: a pair of pincers to fasten the wire in his teeth and a scraper with which to clean his teeth. He wrote this was the only way he could keep using his teeth, for he had little hope of returning to Philadelphia just to have his teeth cleaned. The letter mentioned that a Colonel Harrison would deliver the items to Washington. It went on to say that it would be all right to mail the scraper. He ended the letter by assuring the good dentist that as an honorable man, Washington would pay his dental bill with all promptness.

Well, as luck would have it, the letter never reached Dr. Baker in Philadelphia. Somehow, somewhere, the British intercepted it. And what was the reaction of the English to George Washington's letter to his dentist? Well—

It seems that particular letter created quite a stir. The British general staff just couldn't imagine that the head of an entire army would take time out just before an important battle to write a letter to his dentist. They were certain it was a coded message.

The British top staff spent valuable hours trying to break the code they imagined was in Washington's letter. They even rushed copies off to London to be deciphered. All worked to no avail. The code could not be broken.

Then, on October 6, 1781, General George Washington, dirty teeth and all, attacked Cornwallis and the British at Yorktown. After fourteen days of fighting, Cornwallis surrendered. The colonies became a free and independent nation. And George Washington was finally able to clean and fix his teeth.

A MONUMENT TO A LEFT LEG

*I*t is, undoubtedly, the strangest monument ever erected. It is a memorial to a left leg. It stands in a secluded spot of the Saratoga Battlefields in the state of New York. It is really quite a nice monument.

This testimony to someone's bravery during the revolutionary war is a rather imposing marble slab. A column resembling a Revolutionary cannon is carved on one side. It also shows a wreath, a general's epaulet, and a boot of a left leg.

On the reverse side it reads, "ERECTED BY JOHN WATTS DE PEYSTER, BREVET MAJOR GENERAL: S.N.Y.; 2ND VICE PRESIDENT SARATOGA MONUMENT ASSOCIATION. IN MEMORY OF THE 'MOST BRILLIANT SOLDIER' OF THE CONTINENTAL ARMY WHO WAS WOUNDED ON THIS SPOT, THE SALLY PORT OF BURGOYNES' GREAT (WESTERN)

REDOUBT; 7TH OCTOBER 1777; WINNING FOR HIS COUNTRYMEN THE DECISIVE BATTLE OF THE AMERICAN REVOLUTION AND FOR HIMSELF THE RANK OF MAJOR GENERAL."

But who owned this leg? And if he was so much a hero, why wasn't his name mentioned?

This great military leader was born in 1741, in Norwich, Connecticut. Even as a youth he was rebellious. At the age of fourteen, he ran away to fight in the French and Indian War. Following several battles, he deserted, but he was excused because of his youth.

After working in business for several years, with the outbreak of the Revolutionary War, he became a captain in the Connecticut militia. In 1775, he fought with Ethan Allen and the Green Mountain Boys at Ticonderoga. Later that year, he led 1,000 troops in an unsuccessful attack on Quebec, hoping to make Canada our fourteenth state. Though his left leg was broken, his courage won him a promotion to Brigadier General.

According to Joe Craig, park ranger at the Saratoga National Park, it was his aggressiveness in battle that built his military reputation. It was an aggressiveness that often bordered on rashness, alienating his superiors and his men.

It was on the very spot where the monument had been erected that this soldier wounded his left leg for a second time while beating the British in one of the most decisive battles of the Revolutionary War.

Who was this hero and why was only his left leg honored? Well—

This great Revolutionary War hero who led his troops to one of the most decisive victories in the Revolutionary War was none other than General Benedict Arnold. It seems that despite Congress voting him the country's thanks for his services and promoting him, he felt slighted and decided to join the British.

It wasn't until 1887 that a monument to Arnold's left leg was finally erected. Legend has it that later in the war, while speaking with some American prisoners, Arnold asked the rebels what they would do to him if they captured him. In reply, they said they would cut off his left leg, give it full military honors, and hang the rest of him. As Park Ranger Craig put it, "It's a good thing Arnold met guys who didn't hold a grudge."

A REAL HERO

*T*his person was a doctor, spy, style promoter, social reformer, and the only civilian ever to receive the Congressional Medal of Honor. Oh yes, this person was also a woman!

Mary Edwards Walker was born November 26, 1832, in Oswego, New York. Her father had been one of the leaders in the reform movement in upstate New York. From childhood, Mary was actively involved in working for women's rights, especially the issue of dress reform. Along with Amelia Bloomer and Elizabeth Cady Stanton, she disregarded the corset, which she called a coffin, and took to wearing Turkish pantaloons, which became known as "bloomers." Eventually she became famous for wearing men's full evening dress, which resembled a tuxedo, especially when lecturing on women's rights.

In 1855, Mary was one of the first women in the United States to become a doctor, graduating from Syracuse Medical College. With her husband, Albert Miller, she opened up a joint medical practice in Rome, New York, which eventually failed, as did her marriage.

With the outbreak of the Civil War, Dr. Walker assisted the Union Army and worked in field hospitals, wearing men's clothing. Originally she was only allowed to serve as a nurse. But eventually, she became an assistant surgeon and served with the 52nd Ohio Infantry. Though she was never commissioned, Dr. Walker continued her mode of dress, wore a man's uniform jacket, long trousers, and carried two pistols at all times. She even served with distinction at the battles of Fredericksburg and Chickamauga.

During this time she made several trips into enemy lines to treat civilians and to act as a spy for the North. Unfortunately, during one of these trips, Dr. Walker was captured and imprisoned. She was always proud of the fact that four months later she was traded, *man for man*, for a Confederate officer.

After the war, President Andrew Johnson personally awarded her the Congressional Medal of Honor. For the rest of her eighty-seven years she continued as a doctor, social reformer, journalist, and lecturer.

Then in 1917, along with nine hundred others, her Congressional Medal of Honor was revoked because of lack of War Department Records. The government immediately demanded the return of the medal. Did Dr. Mary Edwards Walker ever give up her medal of heroism? Well—

No way! She proudly wore it every day until her death on February 21, 1919. It can be seen in almost every photo taken of her. For years after her death, her granddaughter waged a campaign to officially reinstate the honor to Dr. Walker. Finally, on June 10, 1977, it was restored by President Jimmy Carter.

Though Dr. Walker literally saved thousands of lives, and led the way for social reforms decades ahead of her time, she died alone and almost penniless.

But this "shocking female surgeon in trousers" was a true American patriot, with great determination and courage. Dr. Mary Edwards Walker was someone to whom we should all be thankful.

A Reporter's Reporter

She was the stuff of which legends are made—but she was no legend. Her real name was Elizabeth Cochrane. The world, however, knew her as Nellie Bly. She was arguably the most famous newspaper reporter of the nineteenth century and the creator of investigative reporting.

Elizabeth was born in a small mill town in Pennsylvania. From a very young age she wanted nothing more than to be a reporter for a newspaper. At the age of seventeen she moved to Pittsburgh to follow her dream.

Dismayed by an editorial in the *Pittsburgh Dispatch* which dealt with women, she wrote a stinging rebuke entitled "What Girls Are Good For." Elizabeth's article repudiated virtually everything in that editorial, line for line, humiliating its author.

Surprisingly, either out of fear or admiration, the newspaper was impressed enough to offer this young lass a job as a reporter. Fearing she might lose her innocence, both literally and figuratively, they wanted to protect her identity. The newspaper had her assume a nom de plume, Nellie Bly.

Nellie immediately began submitting heart wrenching stories about the plight of divorced women. Her writing had a ring of truth. And although it was sharp-tongued and controversial, it did sell newspapers.

Her next foray exposed the conditions in Pittsburgh's slums, sweatshops, and decaying jails. Nellie accomplished this with such vivid details that many of the advertisers complained. In response, the newspaper encouraged her to take a vacation in Mexico.

Before long, Nellie began sending back stories of decadency, debauchery, and corruption from our good neighbor to the south. It took the Mexican government no time at all to very strongly suggest she go home. So she left—with a suitcase full of notes. When questioned by a customs official at the border, she informed him that the suitcase was full of ladies' unmentionables. Perplexed and embarrassed, the officers bypassed any examination of Nellie's luggage.

Arriving back home, Nellie decided Pittsburgh was too tame for her. So off she went to New York City, where she convinced none other than Joseph Pulitzer to hire her.

And how did Nellie Bly do in the big city of New York? Well—

As one might suspect, Nellie took New York by storm. Upon arriving in the Big Apple, she immediately got herself committed to the city's insane asylum for ten days. When she emerged, she wrote of the "human rat hole, cruel nurses, rotting food, and overall filth." The nation was electrified. Soon legislation was passed to improve conditions in the city's many asylums. Using a variety of disguises, she also exposed deplorable prison conditions, corruption in the state legislature, and fraudulent employment agencies.

Many thought her stories were written by a team of brilliant male writers. However, most amazing of all, this quiet, petite, young lady, with sad gray eyes, accomplished all of this before she celebrated her twenty-second birthday.

A SONG FOR DOROTHY

*I*t was to be a first in movie history. Harold Arlen and Yip Harburg had been hired to write an entire score for a movie *before* the shooting even began. This meant every song had to comment on the characters and/or advance the plot. Except for animated cartoons, writing the music first had never been done before.

This musical dealt with L. Frank Baum's classic tale, *The Wizard of Oz*. As part of the $25,000 fee for the project, producers Mervyn Leroy and Arthur Freed wanted the two song writers to create a ballad that would act as a transition from the bland land of Kansas to the colorful world of Oz. They wanted a "song of yearning: to give some emotion to Dorothy's scene of frustration and trouble." Oh, was that all?

Carefully and methodically, Harold Arlan started to put some notes together, but nothing seemed to work. Then one night, while he and his wife, Anya, were driving in to see a movie at Grauman's Chinese Theater, a melody came to him. It was broad and windswept in nature. He parked the car in front of Schwab's Drug Store and began to write.

The next day, when he played the tune for his partner, Kip Harburg, the tune came out very majestic and solemn, almost too solemn. But it just didn't sound like a tune for a thirteen-year-old.

Feeling stumped, they decided to ask their friend, Ira Gershwin, to step in and lend a hand. Gershwin suggested they pick up the tempo and thin out the harmony. It was exactly what the song needed. Harburg sat down and started to spin out a set of lyrics that evolved around a rainbow image. Even though this didn't follow the Kansas part of the story, they truly felt they captured the moment that scene called for.

When the score was completed, producers Leroy and Freed and songsters Arlen and Harburg proudly presented their masterpiece to the executives at MGM, the studio that was producing the picture. And what was their reaction to this newly born classic? Well—

Much to the amazement of all, the executives from MGM absolutely loved the score for *The Wizard of Oz*—all *except* for the tune entitled "Over the Rainbow." Three times they insisted the song be removed. They claimed it would only drag down the tempo of the picture. Finally, an outraged Arthur Freed prevailed, saying, "The song stays, or I go! It's that simple!" The song stayed and the rest, as we say, was history.

Both "Over the Rainbow" and Judy Garland went on to win Oscars. And, as everyone knows, the song became Judy Garland's signature song. When she presented it, sitting on the edge of the stage for her 1967 comeback special, there wasn't a dry eye in the house. What a singer! What a song!

AND A STORY WAS BORN

Robert had been a very sickly child, suffering from a lung disease that eventually developed into tuberculosis. However, he was an avid reader. Robert loved to read literature and history, especially the history of his beloved Scotland. And he was a dreamer. He would spend hours dreaming of the open air, the sea, and all the adventures he would experience when he became a man.

After completing prep school, Robert studied engineering for a while, but he didn't like it. Then, by the age of twenty-five, he became a lawyer, but he didn't like that either. What he really loved was writing. So he began writing short stories, essays, and even a few novels. Shortly after his twenty-sixth birthday he fell head over heels in love.

His romance did have a few minor obstacles. Fanny, his beloved, was an American, had two children, and was already married. But that didn't stop the determined Robert. When he was twenty-nine, over the objections of his parents, he followed Fanny to San Francisco. Upon his arrival, Fanny got a proper divorce, and the two were married. Unfortunately, all this caused Robert's health to worsen.

So, Robert and Fanny packed up the family and moved back to the small village of Braemer, Scotland. But the winters of Scotland were wet and harsh. Robert was forced to spend most of his time indoors tutoring his young stepson in constitutional law.

Being very bored, the young lad begged Robert for something more exciting. So Robert began to spin a yarn about pirates and buried treasure for the lad. He even drew a map of its location. Each day he would weave another part of the story around the map he had drawn. He called his story "The Sea Cook." He tried publishing it in a young folks' magazine—without success. Finally, in 1883, after changing the title, his story was published as a full fledged novel.

And what was the novel that grew out of illness and boredom? Well—

By now you have undoubtedly recognized this novel as Robert Louis Stevenson's *Treasure Island*. Shortly after publishing *Treasure Island*, Stevenson moved his family back to America so he could receive treatment for his tuberculosis. With improved health, he and his family set out on a real adventure, sailing to the South Seas. They settled in Samoa where Robert became a planter and took an active part in local community affairs.

Over time, he became so beloved by the Samoans that upon his death in 1894, the local chiefs buried him on the top of a mountain. His gravestone was inscribed with his poem, "Requiem," whose last lines served as a fitting epitaph for this writer and adventurer. "Here he lies, where he longed to be; home is the sailor, home from the sea, and the hunter, home from the hill."

AND ALONG CAME DIXIE

Whenever someone asks the question, "What was the first truly American form of entertainment?," the first response of many would be to think of jazz or maybe the American musical theatre. But there was another form of entertainment that started over 150 years ago. It was the minstrel show.

This most unique form of merriment had its origins back in the 1840s. It lasted as one of the main types of amusement in the United States until the start of the twentieth century, when it evolved into vaudeville. The first important minstrel company was organized by E. P. Christy. It was called "The Christy Minstrels." Many of the songs written by Stephen Foster were for minstrel shows.

Most of these shows were performed by white entertainers in black face to impersonate African-Americans. Unfortunately, this perpetuated certain negative stereotypes of Blacks that have taken decades to overcome. However, out of this most popular art form came at least one truly great song.

It all started on a Saturday night at Bryant's Theatre in New York City. A popular minstrel entertainer of the period, Daniel Decatur Emmett, had just finished weaving his magical spell for a most appreciative audience. As he began to leave the theatre, the manager called to him, "Hey, Dan, I need a new song by Monday night—and I want a hit." That was only two days away. Where would he come up with the melody and lyrics for a hit song in just two days?

As it happened, the next day it began to rain—all day. That wasn't the best setting for inspiring the writing of a hit song. However, Dan finally forced himself to sit down and start writing.

What came out of that dark and dismal New York day in 1859 was a song that would not only sweep the nation, but would leave its indelible mark on the events of the country forever. What was the name of that song? Well—

As Daniel Decatur Emmett sat there, his thoughts must have turned to his home in the South. He must have started to think "I wish I was in Dixie." As those words ran through his head, he suddenly realized that was his new song. The rest of the heart-felt words flowed out and "Dixie" was born. It was an immediate smash hit. Within days everyone was singing this catchy tune. The people of the South went wild for it.

As for Daniel Decatur Emmett, unfortunately he sold the copyright to "Dixie" for a mere $500. And that was the last penny he would ever earn from this most famous American folk song.

BILLY HAD A SECRET

Billy Lee Tipton had a secret!

Billy was born in 1914 in Oklahoma City. When he moved to Kansas City, it seems as though he developed a love for music, especially jazz. Even at a young age, Billy must have been quite proficient on the piano and saxophone. Though he completed high school, he never requested his graduation documents.

After commencement, he made his way to Spokane, Washington. It was there he pursued a career as a jazz musician, still carrying his secret. Tipton continued to perform in nightclubs throughout the 40s, 50s, and even into the 60s. Quite often he appeared with his own group, "The Billy Tipton Trio." It was later reported, by those who knew him, that he appeared with such name bands of the day as Scott Cameron, Russ Carlyle, and Jack Teagarden, though rarely performing outside the

Pacific Northwest. For over thirty years, Billy Lee Tipton closely guarded his secret.

Billy always seemed to be very conscious of his appearance. His barber later said that Billy was very image conscious and "fussy" about his haircuts. His repair man remembered that Billy always like to appear tall. Because of this, Billy had his shoes built up.

During the 50s, Billy married twice, both for a very short period of time. In 1960, he married Kitty Oakes. They adopted and raised three sons. But this marriage also eventually ended when they divorced in 1979. Billy was quoted as saying, "I never did do too good at picking wives." However, some thought it was his flirtatious ways with the ladies that ended his marriages.

Despite his divorces, Billy seemed to be very loving and caring toward his sons. He even served as their Boy Scout leader. Billy would marry and divorce twice more.

As he grew older, Billy found himself alone, living in a trailer. However, throughout his entire life, he clung tenaciously to his career in music. It was as though jazz was his entire life—more important even than his family.

Then, in 1988, Billy began ailing, suffering from stomach pains. Disregarding the urgings of his children, he staunchly refused to go to a doctor. Finally on January 21, 1989, Billy Lee Tipton died of a bleeding ulcer.

And what was the precious secret that Billy Lee Tipton would not reveal during his life? Well—

It was paramedics who finally discovered Billy Lee Tipton's secret. When they came to tend to this dying man, they discovered that he—was a she! That's right! Billy Lee Tipton was really Dorothy Lucille Tipton.

Apparently, at the age of nineteen, Dorothy decided to take a male identity. For fifty-six years, she successfully fooled her fellow musicians, her three adopted sons, and four of her five wives. Apparently wife number three discovered Tipton's secret, but only after their divorce.

The big question was *why?* It seems that Dorothy truly fell in love with jazz more than anything else.

During the 40s, 50s, and 60s the only hope for a white female in the world of jazz was as a singer. So Dorothy became Billy. Her one adopted son summed it up, "Now I know why I couldn't get him to a doctor—he had so much to protect!"

CLIMBING MOUNT MCKINLEY

Alaska's Mount McKinley must be the crown jewel of the North American continent. Rising to over 20,320 feet of majestic splendor, with temperatures that dropped to -40°, this inactive volcano is the highest summit in North America, and a much sought after goal for mountain climbers. But who conquered it first?

It all started one fateful night in the spring of 1910. A group of local miners were enjoying a few drinks in Billy McPhees's Saloon. In the middle of the ninth or tenth round of beverages, someone asked if anybody could possibly make it to the top of Mount McKinley. McPhee promptly agreed to pay $500 in gold dust to the first person to reach its top.

Brimming with confidence—and whiskey—six sourdough miners decided to take up the challenge. Less than an hour later, with almost no preparation, the six arrived at the foot of Mount McKinley. However, a rather spirited fistfight left only three, Peter Anderson, William Taylor, and Michael McGonnagall, willing, or perhaps able, to begin the climb.

They set out, overflowing with confidence and yet almost totally ignorant of the necessities and skills needed for climbing a mountain of the magnitude of Mount McKinley. This trio did everything wrong. They didn't explore the best route; they brought no spare food, no climbing irons, and didn't even have a rope. They did, however, take along a fourteen-foot flag pole and a flag to perch at the top of the summit to prove their success.

Upon their return to McPhees's Saloon, they told a most heroic tale about how they hacked a stairway out of the icy slope of Karsten's Ridge, waited out blizzards at the 11,000-foot mark, only to find themselves with almost no food left.

Undaunted, they reported how they went on, miraculously, perhaps instinctively, choosing the only practical route up that indomitable mountain. With only four hundred feet to go to the summit, they told how McGonnagall quit, too exhausted to go on.

Anderson and Taylor described their final assault, struggling onward and upward, undeterred, until at last reaching the top. Then, with great bravado, they reenacted the planting of their flag atop the north peak of Mount McKinley.

And did any of their friends back at McPhees's Saloon believe their astonishing tale? Well—

No, not at all! But then, on June 7, 1913, an experienced climbing team, led by Harry Karstens and Rev. Hudson Stuck, reached the summit of the south peak of Mount McKinley. As they stood there, seemingly the first persons ever to behold this most majestic of views, something caught their eye. There, over on the north peak, waving in all its glorious splendor, was the flag and flag pole that Taylor and Anderson had planted some three years earlier.

The fact of whether or not they ever collected their $500 in gold dust from Billy McPhee is lost to history. But the names of Peter Taylor and William Anderson will forever be remembered as the first two individuals to conquer Mount McKinley.

COLUMBUS: FACT OR FICTION

One of the first historical figures many of us learned about is Christopher Columbus. But how much of what we learned is fact? According to the International Columbian Quincentenary Alliance, here is the truth about some of the myths we learned.

Myth number one: Columbus proved the world was round. Wrong. By the end of the fifteenth century almost everyone agreed the earth was round. The big question was in reference to how big the earth was. Columbus underestimated its size by one-fourth.

Myth number two: Queen Isabella sold the crown jewels to pay for his first voyage. Wrong again. She may have suggested it, but she never sold a thing. To pay off a debt to the crown, the town of Palos provided two ships. Most of the other expenses were paid for by private backers.

Myth number three: the initial voyage was perilous, filled with bad weather and lack of food. I'm afraid not. To begin with, Columbus had enough food for an entire year. As for the weather, it was almost perfect for the entire trip, with only an occasional cloud drifting by. As a matter of fact, modern sailors who navigate this same route for the first time are amazed at how easy it is. The return trip was another matter. Columbus and his men ran head long into a fierce hurricane and almost lost both remaining ships.

Myth number four: the priest was among the first to step off the *Santa Maria* onto dry land in 1492. Oh, so wrong. Despite the deep religious convictions of Columbus and his men, there were no priests or friars on any of the ships for that first voyage. They came later.

Myth number five: Columbus had a crew of hundreds of hardened criminals aboard three large, ocean going caravels. Sorry, that's wrong, too. Of the ninety men on that first historic voyage, only four were criminals. The crew manifest consisted of forty sailors aboard the *Santa Maria*, twenty-six on the *Pinta*, and twenty-four on the *Nina*. With the wreck of the *Santa Maria*, the *Nina* and *Pinta* returned to Spain, leaving thirty-nine volunteers behind to hold down the fort. Sadly, they were all killed before Columbus could return.

Myth number six: Columbus discovered North America. You guessed it, wrong again. He never even saw North America. Instead he landed on islands in the Caribbean.

But, what about his death? We certainly know the facts of his death and burial, don't we? Well—

We have heard stories of how Christopher Columbus, discoverer of America, died of syphilis, in chains, penniless, in a Spanish prison, and was buried in the Dominican Republic—correct? Wrong on all counts.

Although some of his men may have brought that feared contact disease back to Europe, there is no record of Columbus ever having contracted it. Though we do not know the exact cause of his death, we do know that Columbus suffered from gout and loss of sight in his later life.

As for his financial status, though he had lost a few privileges at court, he was relatively wealthy and died at home. As for his burial site, today his remains, though moved several times, seem to be spread between Seville, Spain; Santo Domingo, Dominican Republic; and Genoa, Italy. That's Chris, all over.

FATHER KNOWS BEST?

*T*he year was 1899. The United States was about to enter a brand new century. It truly was an age of excitement. Every day seemed to bring some new technological advancement that had been all but unheard of only a few short years before. Ships were powered by steam. The railroad connected every part of this country, north to south, and east to west. The telephone appeared in homes across the nation. There was even talk of a new fangled horseless carriage. The world seemed to be virtually exploding with new advances.

One fair afternoon, two highly distinguished gentlemen sat down for lunch with all of this new technological advancement as a backdrop. During their meal they began to discuss the future of mankind. One was a professor at a small sectarian college. The other man was the bishop of his church.

Almost immediately their highly divergent views became apparent. The professor began predicting that the first half of the new century would bring more and greater inventions than could be dreamed of. He predicted that, in time, man would fly higher and faster than the eagle. The bishop was shocked. He maintained that man's great inventions and material advances had all been made. He insisted that humanity's future task in the new century was to concentrate on growing in grace. As a matter of fact, the good bishop went on to say, "It is given only to God and the angels to fly."

Little did either man realize how soon it would be before the good bishop would be proven wrong. And not only was the bishop totally in error, but, indirectly, he was responsible for proving the total falseness of his prophecy concerning the possibility of man flying.

Who was this bishop? What connection did he have to the development of man's ability to fly? Well—

Not only was that bishop proven wrong, but the proof came much faster than anyone could have imagined.

For it was less than five years later that two bicycle mechanics from Dayton, Ohio, shattered the bishop's prophecy forever. It was on a windy stretch of sand, near Kitty Hawk, North Carolina, that a small group gathered to witness history, the test of a new invention. They watched as a large clumsy contraption, half kite and half box, lurched into the air. They stood there in awe as it stayed aloft for twelve full seconds.

And who was the goodly bishop who predicted "It is given only to God and the angels to fly"? His name was Bishop Milton Wright of Dayton, Ohio, father to Orville and Wilbur Wright, the two brothers who made that first historic flight back in 1903.

GO, TRABI, GO

*I*t is, undoubtedly, the most unique production line automobile ever made. It was, at once, the most loved and the most hated. Even the production workers who put them together made jokes about this most unusual car. They said if it had two tail pipes it would have made a good wheelbarrow. To the world it was known as the Trabant, but to the East Germans it was lovingly referred to as *der Trabi*.

The idea was conceived in pre-World War II Germany. The original Trabant, called the AWZ P70, was intended to be a closed motorbike. With its small engine and lightweight construction, it seemed like a good idea. Like the Volkswagen, the Trabant was designed to be a people's car, but oh, what it turned out to be!

To begin with, its noisy, little twenty-six horse-power engine was called the "little stinker" because it produced thirty times more pollution than a large Mercedes Benz. This diminutive "power plant" was an air-cooled, two-cycle job. It never needed to have its valves adjusted, because it didn't have any valves. It was designed to hold four passengers, provided three of them were midgets, and all were very friendly.

The Trabant didn't include such luxuries as carpeting, a glove box, or even a fuel gauge. Its one creature comfort was a heater, which had two settings—on and off. The heater also had the nasty habit of importing more engine fumes than the exhaust expelled.

Did anyone ever buy any of these mechanical disasters? You bet they did. Buyers waited up to eighteen months to take delivery of this noble chariot. The price was equal to an entire year's salary for an East German. If bought on the black market, the price doubled.

The Trabi began production in 1959, the same year the Russians put their Sputnik into space. As a matter of fact, when translated from German to English, Trabant means "satellite" or "fellow traveler." Since its humble beginning, hundreds of thousands of Trabis were built.

As for the production plant, that was an experience in itself. Located in Zwickau, it was dimly lit and sooty. The main assembly tools needed were a screwdriver and pliers. More often than not, the production line would break down, forcing the workers to push each car from station to station.

As for performance, a Trabi could zoom from zero to sixty in about thirty seconds and reach a top speed of sixty-six miles per hour in less than an hour.

But what was the destiny of this mechanical marvel? Well—

In 1990, *Car and Driver* magazine, having tested a Trabant, reported the following. "The engine provides no braking effect at all. Nor do the brakes!" But despite all, *Car and Driver* made Der Trabi the 1990 car of the year. Why? It was accorded this honor because of all the East Germans it ferried across the border to freedom in the West.

In April of 1991, the last Trabant creaked off the assembly line. Even today, they produce an environmental hazard. It seems the body of the Trabant is made of a mix of phenol plastic and cotton, which, when burned, emits deadly dioxins. A few were ground up and spread on snowy winter roads.

But to those who used *der Trabi* as a chariot to freedom, it will always be the superstar of cars.

HE READ HIS OWN OBITUARY

*I*magine reading not only your own obituary, but also your own epitaph. That's exactly what happened to John Partridge.

John had been born in Ireland in the last half of the seventeenth century. Coming from a rather humble family, he became a cobbler by trade.

Over time John developed a growing interest in astrology. He felt he had a real gift for reading the future in the stars. Before long, in an attempt to supplement his meager cobbler earnings, John became a full-fledged astrologer. He even went so far as to publish his own almanac entitled *Merlinus Libertatus*. Things were looking up for Mr. Partridge.

Then something very bizarre happened. In 1708, a publication started being circulated around his community predicting his death. It stated, "John Partridge would infallibly die upon the twenty-ninth of March next, about eleven at night of a raging fever." The author of this prediction was one Isaac Biskerstaff.

There were only two problems with this prediction. First, John felt very healthy. Second, no one had ever heard of Isaac Bickerstaff.

Then, to make matters worse, on March 30, another pamphlet was circulated stating the prophecy had been fulfilled. According to this latest publication, John had indeed died within four hours of the appointed time. It went on to state that on his deathbed, Partridge confessed to being an imposter.

John immediately put notices in all the papers declaring he was still alive and well. But Isaac Bickerstaff and other writers persisted, saying he was an imposter. His epitaph was even published. "Here five foot deep lyes[sic] on his back, a cobbler, star monger, and quack, who to the stars in pure goodwill, does to his best look upward still."

Before long, John was removed from the stationer's register. This created a real problem for him, for now he could neither vote nor sue anyone. The only good news was that it also meant he wouldn't have to pay taxes.

John sought every clue, hoping to find the culprit, but to no avail. He suspected it had something to do with his relentless attacks on the Church of England, but lacked even a shred of evidence. He spent the next seven years trying to reclaim his identity and discover the perpetrator of the hoax.

Did John ever find out? Well—

Unfortunately, to his dying day, John never found out the truth. In 1717 he went to his grave, still minus an identity or the knowledge of who perpetrated this most perfect of hoaxes. Only then was it disclosed that the author of John Partridge's obituary was none other than Jonathan Swift, who also authored *Gulliver's Travels*.

It seems that being an Anglican minister, Swift decided to do something about Partridge's attacks on the Church of England. So he simply declared him dead, thus making him a non-person.

Though Jonathan Swift will forever be known as a great British author, he should also be remembered as having pulled off the perfect hoax.

HOG CREATES TEXAS

*T*he year was 1841. Texas had just won its hard fought independence from Mexico. They immediately created the Republic of Texas, an independent nation. But, the newly formed country of Texas had some serious problems.

Unfortunately, Texas was broke. They had no money and their citizens were facing constant threats of raids from Mexico and from Native Americans. But Texas forged on and held its first national election. They elected Sam Houston as president and voted to join the United States of America. Seeing the creation of this new nation, France and England both wanted Texas to remain independent. They feared the United States would gain more power in the Southwest.

The French government decided to take advantage of the Texans' need for money and offered to loan Texas $5 million, hoping that eventually France might be able to annex Texas into part of the French Empire. To this end, France sent Count Alphonse De Saligny to Texas to negotiate a treaty.

In those days, foreign dignitaries traveled with everything they might need for their comfort and livelihood: horses, food, linens, fodder for the livestock—everything. All of this was to be stored by any inn where they stayed.

When they arrived in Austin, Texas, the count, and his entourage of servants, took lodging at the very fashionable establishment called Bullock's Inn. Negotiations between the count and the Texans were going along as smooth as can be, the loan was about to be granted and the treaty ratified, when suddenly, something went horribly wrong.

It seems that the innkeeper's hog had broken into the storage room that housed the count's provisions, and, when finally found out, was gorging himself on the corn stored there for the Frenchman's horse. Upon catching the offending swine in the act, one of the count's servants promptly killed the offending hog. This prompted the innkeeper Bullock, owner of the hog, to trounce the count's servant and throw him out of the inn.

At this point, diplomatic relations broke down, completely. The count refused Bullock's personal apology and demanded instead an apology to France from the Texas secretary of state. And what became of the undiplomatic hog's fax paus? Well—

There they were. The count was demanding a full apology to France from Texas for having his servant thrown out of the inn, while the innkeeper wanted payment for his slain hog. Did those proud Texas senators apologize? Not on your life! They even declined to ratify the treaty. As for the count, he wrote a nasty letter denouncing Bullock and his hog. He then got permission from Paris to deny the loan and returned home, one very angry Frenchman.

As for those Texans, they immediately began negotiations once more with the United States and within a short time became the twenty-eighth state of the Union. All because of a French count, some corn, and a hog.

HUGH WILLIAMS' SAGA

*I*t is perhaps one of the most beautiful straits in the world. It is unquestionably one of the most gorgeous bodies of water in or around the British Isles. It is called the Menai Strait.

Located off the southwestern shores of Wales, the Menai Strait is a narrow strip of seawater, about fifteen miles long that separates the Island of Anglesey from the mainland of Wales. Its narrowest point is only about 550 yards wide, and it can go from a placid calm to a raging torrent of tides and winds, seemingly in a matter of moments.

In addition to being a place of beauty, inspiration, and respect, the Menai Strait has also played an important part in the history of Wales. It was there that the Druids made their last stand against the invading Roman army centuries ago.

But most remarkable of all, the Menai Strait is the site of one of the most incredible set of coincidences ever to occur since man first set to sea.

It all started on a cold and stormy December 5, in the year 1664. A ship was cautiously trying to make its way through this most treacherous of passages. Suddenly, it began to founder. Almost within moments it was lost, with all eighty-one persons aboard drowned—all that is, save one; his name was Hugh Williams.

One hundred twenty-one years were passed. The date was December 5, in the year 1785. Once more the tumultuous power of the Irish Sea's December winds roared through the Menai Strait. Another vessel attempted to make a night passage through this valley of death when it sank. All sixty of its passengers and crew were plunged into the icy cold waters, which raged with the rising tide. When the sun rose, only one survivor was to be found. His name—Hugh Williams.

The coincidence was astonishing. Two vessels sunk at exactly the same spot in the same strait, both on the fifth of December. And in each case the only survivor was a man named Hugh Williams.

Is there more to this sea tale? Well—

Just thirty-five years later, on August 5, in the year 1820, a third ship was sent to the bottom in almost the identical spot in the Menai Strait. This time twenty-four crew members lost their lives to the sea. The twenty-fifth member of the crew was the only survivor. And his name? You guessed it—Hugh Williams.

Imagine, if you can, the odds of this occurring. Three different vessels, all sunk on the fifth of the month (albeit different months), at exactly the same location, in that small strait off the southwest coast of Wales. And in each case, the sole survivor was a man named Hugh Williams.

Now, I won't say that I am a believer in fate, *but*, if I ever find myself about to sail through the Menai Strait on the fifth of the month, I think I'll change my name to "Hugh Williams."

INSTANT CITY, ANYONE?

*J*ust imagine, at 9:00 a.m. it was nothing more than a set of railroad tracks and an open prairie. By 9:00 p.m. that same day, just twelve short hours later, it was a town with over 10,000 residents. How could that happen?

The date was April 22, 1889. Prior to that time, this entire area had been known as "Indian Land." For as far as the eye could see, only Native Americans were allowed to settle. Then, President Harrison declared that at the strike of noon that day, this territory would be opened to settlement by anyone.

With that, people came by the thousands. Mainly poor and illiterate immigrants, they all wanted a piece of free land. They were looking to seek their fortune in pursuit of the great American dream.

It was the responsibility of the cavalry to hold them back until the appointed time. Then, at precisely twelve noon, the army trumpets blew and the race was on for thousands of land hungry settlers.

They took off by train, wagon, and carriage and even on foot. Each one was eager to lay claim to a parcel of land they hoped would bring them fortune and the good life. By the end of the next day there were stores, saloons, churches, a brothel, and even a school. Most of the settlers had to reconcile themselves to living and working in tents for a while.

However, one entrepreneur, Henry Overholser, anticipated the housing problem. Within days he had eight prefabricated buildings brought in all the way from Minnesota, one of which became the town opera house. The first bank in town started out in the back of a wagon, but soon grew to the largest bank in town.

Some tried to hide in gullies and ravines in order to sneak in to claim land early. They were called *Sooners*, a name used to this day by local sports teams. Interestingly, despite the fact there was no formal law, there was very little crime. However, within forty-eight hours, a community committee of fourteen was set up to settle all disputes.

And what was this city that sprang up over night? Well—

According to Max Nichols of the state historical society, that was how Oklahoma City, the capital of Oklahoma, was born.

Since that day, over a century ago, Oklahoma City has grown to a population of over one million residents and is still growing. The center of town still has the same layout that was set up in 1889. The First National Bank, that started in the back of a wagon and grew to the largest in town, has since disappeared, swallowed up by another bank.

But Oklahoma City is booming, with an expanding economy. It is also becoming known as one of the cultural centers of the Southwest. And all of that truly boomed into existence in just a single day.

IT'S HOW COLD?

*H*aving been born and raised in a Minnesota, Scandinavian family, I have long since accepted the fact that a certain amount of suffering should be looked upon with a point of pride. I well remember, as a youth, hearing the phrase, "That's nothing; when I was young..." which was always followed with a graphic description of the hottest, coldest, wettest, or snowiest day the world had ever seen. And it always just happened to have occurred in southeastern Minnesota.

Of course, I have never been guilty of this kind of action with my own children, but it did get me to thinking: What are some of the weather records that have been recorded on this fine planet of ours? And how did my beloved Minnesota actually stack up with the verified world records? For the answers, I went to a world almanac.

I started with the hottest temperature: Minnesota, +114 degrees Fahrenheit; Asisia, Libya, +136 degrees Fahrenheit (in the shade). Now that's hot!

Certainly Minnesota must be close to the record for coldest: Minnesota, -60 degrees; Vostoc, Antarctica, -129 degrees. Now that's what I call suffering weather.

Then I found out that Minnesota couldn't even lay claim to the largest sudden drop in temperature. That distinction goes to Browning, Montana. In a single twenty-four-hour period, the temperature there dropped from +44 degrees to -56 degrees, a change of 100 degrees. There goes any aspiration I may have had for moving to Montana.

The rainiest day went to the village of Cilaos on an island off the eastern shore of Africa. In a mere twenty-four hours, they experienced over six feet of rain, and ended up with a total of eight feet in forty-eight hours. I hope they had an ark.

For annual rainfall, the record goes to Lioro, Columbia, in South America. This city gets an average of 523.6 inches of rain per year. That is over forty-three feet of water. What a place to sell umbrellas!

Of course, with over 10,000 lakes, I knew Minnesota wouldn't qualify for the driest spot on planet Earth. That distinction goes to Arica, Chile, located in the Atacama Desert of South America. Over the last sixty years, it has averaged only 0.03 inches of precipitation every twelve-month period. Once it went fourteen years between rainfalls. I'm getting thirsty just thinking about it.

I started getting desperate. There must be some meteorological record that Minnesota could claim with pride. Then it hit me. Could our "Star of the North" be the snowiest location in the entire world? Well—

Unfortunately, no. The distinction for the snowiest day goes to Silver Lake, Colorado. In a mere twenty-four hours, they had to dig out from under six feet of the fluffy white stuff.

Minnesota didn't even qualify for the greatest annual snowfall. That award goes to Paradise Ranger Station on Mount Rainer in the State of Washington.

In 1971, they received 1,122 inches of snow. A quick trip to my calculator tells me that's over ninety three feet. Uffda, that's a lot of shoveling.

Finally, what was the furthest south that it snowed? In January 1977, snow was recorded in Homestead, Florida, twenty-five miles south of Miami. It was so unusually cold, they had to bring heat lamps into the Miami Zoo to warm up the iguana.

I guess the weather in Minnesota isn't so bad after all.

LE GENTIL

*I*t seems as though we are forever reading about scientists who have had incredible timing or had a series of unbelievable coincidences which led them to make remarkable discoveries. But have you ever wondered about the poor schmuck who experienced just the reverse? This is his story and it's true.

He was a French astronomer. His entire moniker would take up half this page, so I'll just use his last name, Le Gentil. The year was 1760. He had just learned that Venus was going to make an infrequent pass between Earth and the sun the following year. He was informed that the best location on Earth to observe this natural phenomenon was in India. Wanting to be there in plenty of time, he immediately booked passage for the sub-continent.

The trip was terribly hot and uncomfortable. Eventually, he arrived, only to have his ship barred from entering the Indian port because of a war with

England. This delay caused Le Gentil to miss the passage of Venus.

Undaunted, he decided to stay and wait for the next scheduled passage of that planet—June of 1769. This gave him eight full years to prepare. He was determined to be ready this time. First, he learned the language of the local people. Next, he began building a complete observatory, equipped with all the latest, necessary equipment. Le Gentil tested and retested each piece exhaustively. He was finally ready. He waited. At long last that much anticipated day arrived.

The dawn broke with a bright and clear sky. Le Gentil readied himself mentally and physically. But then, just as Venus was about to pass in front of the sun, out of nowhere, a huge black cloud suddenly appeared on the horizon. It moved swiftly and, at the precise moment for which he had so patiently waited those many years, the sun was completely obscured. When the sky finally cleared, the transit of Venus was completed. All of those years of preparation and work were wasted!

And did this ill-fated scientist ever have a change of luck? Well—

Understandably, this final disappointment was more than he could take. In despair, Le Gentil returned to France, hoping to find some consolation in his homeland.

Incredibly, during his long trip home, faced with turbulent storms and violent seas, he was almost shipwrecked twice. Finally, in 1774, a full fourteen years after he left, he returned to his beloved Paris, home at last—only to discover that he had been declared legally *dead*.

Perhaps it was understandable. After all, there had been no news of his well-being during his entire, lengthy absence. But the worst of it came when he discovered that he had been replaced in the Academy of Sciences *and* his entire fortune had been irrevocably distributed among his heirs.

Now, that is what I call one very unlucky man!

LINCOLN'S FIRST VICTORY

*S*ometimes humor can come from the most unusual situation and at the most unexpected time. That's what happened to President Abraham Lincoln in the spring of 1863, one of the darkest times of his presidency.

Though the confederates had closed to within a day's ride of the nation's capital, for many of the residents in Washington, D.C., the line between friend and foe often blurred. It was not uncommon for them to have friends in both the North and the South. This was especially true for a seamstress named Clara and her husband, Charlie. With Clara having been raised in the state of New York and Charlie growing up in Maryland, they had friends and family on both sides of the battle lines.

However, things became even more complicated for this particular couple. You see, Clara was the personal hat maker for Mary Todd Lincoln, the wife of the president. And Charlie, an ardent abolitionist, had volunteered to be a spy for the North. With many friends in Virginia and Maryland, it was very easy for Charlie to make trips back and forth across enemy lines without arousing suspicion. He would carry messages each way in a fake heel in his boot.

With confederate troops having advanced through Maryland, Virginia, and up into Pennsylvania, it was imperative for Lincoln and his generals to get information about the Confederate army's strength and location.

Charlie was called upon to go to Virginia and bring back this information. In an attempt to look as inconspicuous as possible, he decided to take his wife and new baby along.

Setting out in an open carriage, the three were allowed to pass through the union lines without any problems. However, upon reaching the confederate checkpoint, they were stopped by a rebel blockade and interrogated.

While one soldier did the questioning, another soldier, standing off to the side, noticed a bag Clara had securely tucked under the front seat of the carriage. Before she or Charlie could react, the soldier lunged forward and snatched that precious bag, much to the horror of Clara. With a knowing look, he pulled open the bag and thrust his arm in up to the elbow. And what did he discover, neatly packed in this bag? Well—

With Charlie maintaining stony silence and Clara gasping in horror, that confederate soldier thrust his arm into that bag up to the elbow only to discover it was filled—*with dirty diapers*. Charlie and Clara were allowed to proceed without any further questions.

Upon their safe return to Washington, Clara related the story of their adventure with the confederate soldier and the diaper bag to Mrs. Lincoln, who in turn told her husband, the president. Upon hearing this, President Lincoln was said to have slapped his thigh, let out a laugh that was alleged to have been heard across the Potomac, and said, "Well, I'll be dammed! That's the first time during this entire war that a Yankee's been able to crap on a Confederate!"

Just for the record, Charlie and Clara's last name was—Wolfram. In fact, they were my great grandparents.

MAN'S BEST FRIEND?

I promise that I will be discreet, but I must tell, there is one household item that has always held my fascination. Though it's been around for over 10,000 years and is a daily part of each of our lives, we seem to have a problem talking about it. Of course, I am referring to the lowly toilet.

The toilet has always played a critical part in human hygiene, yes, even the development of civilization throughout history. The first use of a separate room in a house for this specific purpose can be traced all the way back to the year 8000 BC.

It was on the island of Orkney, just off the coast of Scotland. The residents there had stone huts which were equipped with a drainage system to carry human waste down to a nearby stream. By 2500 BC certain areas of India had developed the same system with the waste from each home flowing into a main drain.

85

The flush toilet can be dated back 3,000 years to an island in the Persian Gulf. And just like today, governments eventually became involved. It was in 70 AD when the Roman Emperor Vaspasian levied the first tax on toilets.

But then, for some unknown reason, toilets seemed to have fallen out of favor. Perhaps it was the tax. In 1214 AD, the first public toilets, which, by the way, were coed, were constructed in Europe. Despite their popularity, chamber pots seemed to have been the facility of choice, especially during the night time. Officially, the contents of those chamber pots were supposed to be picked up every day by a waste man. Unfortunately, often as not, they were merely emptied out the nearest window.

In 1596, an Englishman, J. D. Harrington, invented the very first known water closet, but it never caught on. It was Alexander Cumming, in 1775, who introduced England to the first flush toilet that included a trap. But it wasn't until the cholera epidemics of the 1830s that people finally started taking toilets and sanitation seriously. In 1859, Queen Victoria had a gold plated toilet installed, only to have it replaced by the first ceramic stool in 1889. Still there was no rush to flush.

Finally, in 1880, the Scott brothers started mass marketing Waldorf toilet tissue. At long last the indoor flush toilet began gaining its rightful respect around the world. But do you know what great man's father got into trouble for *not* using the toilet? Well—

The year was 1552. The place was a small village about ninety miles north of London. It seems that John, a local glove maker, was fined two shillings for "Making a dung heap in the street." He paid the fine and even went on to be elected Lord High Bailiff of the Village of Stratford-upon-Avon. That's right. It was John Shakespeare, father of William Shakespeare.

If you want to learn more facts about the lowly toilet, stop in and visit the Sulabh International Museum of Toilets the next time you are in India.

MIKE LOSES HIS HEAD

We've all heard the expression "...running around like a chicken with its head cut off." But does a chicken really do that? And if it does, what is the longest it has ever happened? Would you believe a year and a half? That's right. The chicken's name was Mike and it all started on September 10, 1945, in Fruita, Colorado.

That was the day that a local farmer, Lloyd Olsen, found out his mother-in-law was coming for supper. Wanting to make a good impression, he decided to feature one of his prize Wyandotte roosters as the entrée for that evening's meal. His wife, Clara, was famous for her fried chicken.

Lloyd proceeded to pick out a prime five-and-a-half-month old rooster that seemed perfect for the occasion. Knowing his mother-in-law's favorite part of the chicken was the neck, he carefully lined up the ax in an attempt to provide an ample neck bone. With great precision, he hit his mark and off popped the head. Then, as sometimes happens with newly decapitated poultry, the chicken began to stagger around.

At that moment, a strange thing happened. Instead of graciously dropping dead, as any respectable chicken should have done under those circumstances, this feisty foul fluffed up his feathers and seemed to ignore the trauma that had just befallen him. He then began to prance around the barnyard, making pecking motions for food. He even tried to crow.

When the next morning came and Lloyd found this rambunctious rooster still as lively as ever, he decided to give it some help. With an eyedropper, he started putting feed and water directly into its gullet. It took him no time at all to realize he had something special in this chicken.

Lloyd decided to name the headless wonder chicken "Mike" and promptly took Mike on tour. For twenty-five cents each, people from New York to San Diego lined up to see this phenomenon of nature. And Mike flourished through it all, growing from two-and-a-half pounds to nearly eight pounds. He was described as "…a robust chicken…a fine specimen…happy as any other chicken, except, he didn't have a head." His seemingly excellent health perplexed even animal activists.

And what finally happened to "Mike, The Headless Chicken Wonder?" Well—

For a while it looked like he was destined for fame and fortune. He was written up in *Life* and *Time* magazines. He even made it into the *Guinness World Book of Records* and was insured for $10,000.

But, alas, his fame and fortune were fleeting. For only eighteen months after the loss of his head, poor Mike choked to death on a kernel of corn in an Arizona motel.

However, his fame lives on. Every year, on the third weekend in May, Fruita, Colorado, his home town, celebrates "Mike, The Headless Chicken Days." Of course, there is a chicken cook-off and a chicken dance marathon. But what is the featured event? Of course. The "Run Like A Chicken With Your Head Cut Off 5K Race."

NOW THAT WAS A MARATHON

*T*he marathon race is considered by many the noblest of all races. Legend has it that this forty kilometer event dates back to 499 BC. Today it is considered very prestigious just to *complete* this greatest of all races.

But no marathon was more unusual than the one at the 1904 modern day olympic games held in St. Louis, Missouri. It may not have been one for the record books, but it was, indeed, memorable.

It was probably the worst day imaginable for any race: humid and temperature exceeding ninety degrees.

The course was completely unpaved. The runners were preceded not only by horsemen clearing the way, but also by doctors, judges, and reporters, all in automobiles, leaving huge plumes of choking dust and smoke to be inhaled by the competitors.

With President Roosevelt's daughter, Alice, there to honor the winner, the first man crossed the finish line. He was Fred Lorz from New York City. As Alice Roosevelt was about to crown him with a wreath of laurels, someone discovered that, because of cramps, Lorz had hitched a ride in a car for eleven miles, even waving to the crowd from the car, until it overheated. He was immediately disqualified. Even though he was banned from amateur athletics for life, only a year later he was allowed to run in—and win—the Boston Marathon.

The next to cross the finish line was British-born Thomas Hicks who was running as an American. It seems that around the ten-mile mark, Hicks laid down, begging to quit. Instead his trainers forced him to drink strychnine sulfate mixed with raw egg whites, not just once, but several times. And they had him wash it down with brandy. Near death, Hicks was actually half carried across the finish line by his two trainers. Because his feet were still moving, he was declared the winner. It took four doctors to ultimately revive him.

Though all racial minorities had been banned from these games, two black Africans did run in the marathon. But these two weren't originally in town to run in the olympics. They were college students who had been hired to appear as Zulu warriors in a Boar War exhibit at the St. Louis World's Fair that happened to be held at the same time. Though placing ninth and twelfth, these inexperienced runners probably would have done much better had they not been chased over a mile off course by an overly protective guard dog. But was the best yet to come? Well—

To finance his trip to the olympic games, a Cuban postman named Felix Carvajal was forced to run around the main square in Havana and jump up on a box and plead for money. When he had enough funds, he left for the games, only to lose every penny in a crap game in New Orleans. Flat broke, he hitch-hiked to St. Louis, which was a real trick in 1904.

Arriving just in time for the games, Carvajal found he had no running gear. Undaunted, he cut the sleeves off his shirt and the legs off his pants, put on his street shoes, and pronounced himself ready. During the race,

Felix seemed to be tireless, often running backwards while talking to the crowd. But then, overcome by hunger, he detoured into an orchard and ate numerous green apples which gave him stomach cramps. Incredibly, Felix still finished fourth.

OVERCOMING ALL ODDS

*I*n the early age of aviation, this had to have been one of the most historic, yet least heralded, events to take place. It was one of the very first attempts to fly across this vast nation of ours, coast to coast, from New York City all the way to Los Angeles. Today this trip is commonplace, taken by thousands of people each day. But not then!

The year was 1911, less than eight short years after the Wright brothers made their historic first flight. The pilot was a thirty-two-year-old named Galbraith Perry Rogers. He had actually learned to fly from the Wright brothers themselves. His plane was an original Wright biplane.

To say that Rogers had to make this trip by the seat of his pants is an understatement. He had no decent charts or maps and almost no instruments. As for landing fields, they were almost non-existent.

His plan was to follow railroad tracks across the wide expanse of our nation. It sounded like a good idea. But this poor fellow had no idea of the perils that lie ahead of him. The only thing he really did have going for him was his determination.

So, on September 17, 1911, he took off from a small grass field near New York City, only to crash into a tree near Middletown, New York. More determined than ever, he soon had the plane repaired and was back in the air once more, only to almost destroy the plane in a crash near Elmira, New York. But this was just the beginning.

In Salamanca, Rogers hit a barbed wire fence and crashed again near Hornell. Four accidents and he hadn't even left the state of New York!

Rogers, however, was prepared. He had made provision for a car and a train to follow him the entire way. In actuality, these combined to create a complete repair shop on wheels. In no time at all he had the plane repaired and got back in the air—*only to crash once more*! But on he flew. In Indiana, a crash almost completely destroyed the plane yet again. It did not, however, dampen Rogers' spirit. Twice he broke a piston and once he even fell out of the plane, two hundred feet in the air, only to have it crash yet again. And did this daredevil ever make it to sunny California? Well—

As a matter of fact he did. On December 10, almost three months after his initial takeoff, he landed what was left of his plane in Long Beach, California.

The trip covered 4,231 miles, required sixty-eight stops, and featured fifteen crashes. When he landed in California, there was hardly a single original part left on his plane. When he totaled it up, he discovered that the parts he used to repair his plane during the flight could have built four entire new planes.

And so history was made. The first transcontinental airplane flight was completed in eighty-four days.

How long does it take to make that flight today?—about five-and-a-half hours.

OUR PRESIDENT #11½

*I*f I were to ask you to name the eleventh president of the United States, you would answer, "James K. Polk." If I asked you to name the twelfth president of the United States, your answer would be, "Zachary Taylor." But what would your answer be if I were to ask you, "Who was president of the United States number eleven and a half?" Hmmm? Is that your final answer? That was my answer, too, eleven and a half? That was my answer until I ran across the name of David Rice Atchison.

The date of this historic happening was Saturday, March 3, 1849. At the stroke of midnight that evening President James K. Polk's term came to an end. On the next day, General Zachary Taylor was to take his oath of office.

There was only one problem. The next day, March fourth, was a Sunday. Now General Taylor, being a strict Episcopalian, refused to take the oath of office on the Sabbath. He insisted the government would just have to wait until Monday. Ok, no problem. In a case such as this, the presidency automatically reverts to the vice president. Unfortunately, the vice president, George Dallas, had resigned as president of the Senate and his term as vice president expired along with President Polk. Now what?

Fortunately one of the last things the Senate of the Thirtieth Congress did before it adjourned was to re-elect their president pro tem, David Rice Atchison, a senator from Missouri. This automatically made him next in line for the presidency.

Was Senator Atchison legally president for that day? Some say no because he was not legally sworn into office. However, in a 1913 publication entitled, *Biographical Congressional Directory*, it stated that Atchison was "…legal president of the United States for one day."

Then, in 1928, several politicians, including the governor of Missouri, descended upon Plattsburg, Missouri, Atchison's final home. It was there they dedicated a statue to "President Atchison" for his brief term as our nation's leader.

And what did Atchison think about this whole matter? It all depended upon when you asked him. On one occasion, he agreed that he probably was the president for twenty-four hours. However, later he had serious doubts as to whether he would have been allowed to make any major decisions.

And what exactly did President Atchison achieve during his one-day presidency? Well—

Not one single thing! Oh, a few of his colleagues suggested to him that he might make some political appointments. However, he passed on the opportunity.

In actuality, he spent most of his twenty-four-hour tenure as president of the United States of America—*asleep*. As he later told a St. Louis newspaper reporter, "I went to bed. There had been two or three busy nights finishing up the work of the Senate, and I slept most of that Sunday."

Ironically, history was to repeat itself, in a way. Four years later, when Vice President-elect William

R. King died of tuberculosis, Atchison was still president pro tem of the Senate. So, under the articles of the Constitution, he unofficially succeeded King as vice president for nine months. There is no report of how much of this term he slept away.

QUEEN OF THE QUILL

She was called "a legend," "electrifying," "flamboyant," and "ahead of her time." She was the first female stock broker and banker on Wall Street, the first publisher to print Karl Marx's *Communist Manifest*, and the first woman to run for president of the United States. Do you remember reading about her in your high school history classes? No? Well, her name was Victoria Claflin Woodhull.

She was born into her family's traveling medicine show in 1832 in the town of Homer, Ohio. While still in her twenties, she divorced a drunken and abusive husband, and set out on her own.

At the age of thirty, Victoria and her sister, Tennessee Claflin, invaded the wild world of finance by becoming the first female stock brokers and bankers Wall Street had ever seen. They quickly turned a $7,000 loan from Cornelius Vanderbilt into a $700,000 fortune.

Never lacking for courage, this single parent of two next decided to take on the biggest game in town. She ran for the president of the United States. In addition to advocating women's suffrage, she strongly supported short skirts, spiritualism, free love, vegetarianism, birth control, and prostitution. Needless to say, she lost.

It was at this time that Victoria and her sister decided to enter the rugged world of journalism by starting their own newspaper. They soon became known as the "Queens of the Quill" because of their exposés on stock swindles, insurance frauds, and corrupt congressional land deals.

But above all else, their newspaper addressed the issues that concerned women's rights with unusual frankness for that time period. They promoted a vision that women could, and should, live as men's equals in the work place, political arena, church, and even the bedroom. This was outright heresy for that day and age.

They even took on the most famous religious leader of the time, Reverend Henry Ward Beecher. The righteous Reverend Beecher was not only the brother of Harriet Beecher Stowe, but also the great proponent of puritanical living.

All this did not stop them from disclosing the Reverend's various sexual peccadilloes, including a tryst with the wife of his best friend, parishioner, and biographer, Theodore Tilton.

And whatever happened to our nation's first truly emancipated woman? Well—

Not surprisingly, the "Queens of the Quill" and their newspaper soon became the target of "reformer" Anthony Comstock. After spending several weeks in jail and paying out over $60,000 in bail, they were found innocent of all charges.

Victoria then decided to launch into a public speaking career. She held audiences spellbound, despite being called "Mrs. Satan."

Unfortunately, this glorious comet then began to fade. Burned out, Victoria and her sister moved to England, married wealthy men, and lived out the rest of their lives in comfort and quiet obscurity. Victoria died in 1927 at the age of eighty-eight.

In her life, she tried to use the existing laws and political system to create a more egalitarian society. She left a legacy well worth remembering!

THE ARMAGEDDONS OF HISTORY

*A*rmageddon! The end of the world! People have been trying to predict its exact time and date almost since the beginning of recorded time.

One of the earliest to put pen to paper and come up with an exact date on the liquidation of our fair planet was the infamous sixteenth century French prophet and astrologer, Nostradamus. He insisted the world would end when Easter fell on April twenty-fifth. To date, he has been wrong in 1666, 1734, 1886, and 1943. His next chance is 2038.

In 1919, there was an expert meteorologist and seismologist in San Francisco by the name of Albert Porta. Dr. Porta gained fame for his accuracy in predicting earthquakes. Then he caught the country's attention when he announced that on December 17, 1919, there would be a conjunction of six planets. This, he insisted, would create a gigantic magnetic current which would cause the sun to explode and engulf the earth.

When many other scientists agreed that the alignment would occur, hysteria spread throughout the world. After tense days of waiting, the fatal day arrived; the planets lined up—but nothing happened. So Albert Porta went back to predicting weather, hopefully, with more accuracy.

In 1925, a young girl in Los Angeles announced the Archangel Gabriel had told her the world would end at midnight on Friday, February 13, 1925. A house painter named Robert Reidt in Long Island immediately jumped into action. He took out ads in all the New York papers telling all who would listen to meet him on a mountain top at the appointed hour of doom.

At the stroke of midnight, all those who had assembled, clad in white muslin, threw up their hands and cried out, "Gabriel, Gabriel!" But once more nothing happened. Then Reidt informed them that the prediction had been made in relation to midnight Pacific time. Confidently, they all sat down and waited another three hours. Still nothing! As he went down the mountain he was heard to say that it was all spoiled by the flashbulbs of the photographers.

Mr. Reidt, however, would not give up. Twice more he assembled his faithful following on that mountain top to await the Armageddon. When his third attempt failed in 1932, he decided to forsake his doomsday calling and seek other employment.

There is an old Roman adage that states "Rome and the world are safe, so long as the Coliseum stands." When huge cracks appeared in 1954 throughout that 1800-year-old amphitheatre, thousands panicked, despite reassurances from the Vatican. As the deadly hour of doom came and went, the Prelate of Rome was proven right, everyone went home and builders repaired the cracks.

But what do the scientists have to say about the end of the world? Well—

World scientists have calculated from fossil records that comets have hit the earth every ten to thirty million years. Some researchers, from the Harvard-Smithsonian Center of Astrophysics, claim that a six-mile wide comet, similar to the one they feel destroyed the dinosaurs, will again hit our fair planet. They project this comet will have a velocity of one hundred times a speeding bullet and the explosive force of 100 million tons of TNT. When this comet collides with earth, continents will tumble and a three mile high tidal wave will engulf all living things. The date of this occurrence: April 14, 2126. I'm putting that date on my calendar!

THE BOY WHO LOVED
BUFFALO BILL

Count Felix von Luchner was much like any thirteen-year-old boy growing up in Dresden, Germany, better than average student, liked outdoor sports, and loved to read.

Then one day, he started reading a book that would forever change his life. It was the exciting tale of William Cody, known around the world as Buffalo Bill. Felix made up his mind, right then and there, that he was going to go to America and meet Buffalo Bill. Of course there was only one obstacle—his mother said NO!

Despite her objections, he proceeded with his plan, left home, and headed for Hamburg. Upon his arrival, he began wandering the docks until he finally signed up as a cabin boy aboard a Russian freighter, the *Niobe*. It was bound for America, by way of Australia. But the voyage proved to be very harsh, indeed. The young count was beaten, overworked, underfed, and scared most of the voyage. At one point he even fell out of the rigging into the sea. He only kept from drowning, because of exhaustion, by grabbing the legs of an albatross that had swooped down for a view. By some miracle, he was able to hold on to that startled bird until a rescue boat arrived.

Upon reaching Australia, he jumped ship and wandered Brisbane for several months. Finally, he signed on an American ship, *Golden Shore*, which took him to San Francisco. When Felix arrived in the city by the bay, he was told Buffalo Bill lived in Denver. He was told to get to Denver, he would have to follow the railroad tracks, *walking the ties*, a distance of 1,300 miles.

With renewed vigor, he set out to do just that. Though he did catch an occasional passing freight train, he ended up walking most of the way. At long last, after numerous detours, sailing over 12,000 miles, and walking almost 1,800 miles, there he stood at the door of his idol, Buffalo Bill Cody. Sadly, it was then he found out that Buffalo Bill was in *Germany* and at that very moment *was a guest in his father's house in Dresden*.

Did Count Felix von Luckner ever meet his idol, Buffalo Bill Cody? Well—

Eventually, Felix made his way back to Germany. When World War I broke out, he entered the German navy and was made commandant of the vessel, *Seeadler*. Before the war was over, he was responsible for the sinking of thirty-five Allied vessels. But most amazingly of all, because of the great love and respect he had for America and its people, not a single person from any of those ships lost their lives.

Word of his deeds spread throughout the United States. When the war ended, three different American cities made Count Felix von Luchner an honorary citizen. Ironically, however, he never did get to meet his hero, Buffalo Bill Cody.

THE CONVICT SHIP

At one time, it was advertised as the oldest merchant ship afloat, with a most unique history. She was the sailing vessel HMS *Success*.

Originally, she was built for Cockerell and Company of Calcutta, India. Massive in construction, her hull was primarily made out of enduring Burmese teak. But perhaps her most distinctive feature was her peculiar arrow-shaped sails.

Initially, the *Success* was employed in carrying cargo around India. Then, in 1792, she was sold to the Frederick Mangus & Company of London, England, who put her to work for the next fifty years hauling immigrants to Australia. In 1845, she started hauling cargo once more.

It was at this point her destiny seemed to change. In 1852, the *Success* was purchased by the State of Victoria in Australia. Initially she was used as a women's prison; but she then became a "reformatory ship for seamen."

Before long, stories started to circulate about the horrors committed to those prisoners aboard. They spoke of unbelievable atrocities. The state tried to subdue the uproar by converting the HMS *Success* into a floating explosives warehouse, but the public outrage continued.

Finally, in 1885, to end the unpleasant chapter in Australian history, the state ordered the HMS *Success* scuttled, sunk in one of its harbors. But that was not to be the end of the once magnificent ship.

In 1890, at the ripe old age of one hundred, she was brought up from her watery grave. Some local entrepreneurs purchased the rights to the *Success* and re-floated her. Finding her in remarkably good condition, she was refitted and turned into a floating exhibit as the "Convict Ship."

After five years on display in Australia, she sailed to Europe where she toured for another twenty years. Then in 1912, the *Success* caught the eye of two enterprising Americans who purchased her, had her re-rigged yet again as a four-masted barkentine, and sailed her to Boston.

For twenty-two years she entertained visitors from New England to San Francisco. She even made an appearance at the great Chicago World's Fair in 1933.

And what finally happened to this once proud and noble sailing vessel, which was billed as the oldest merchantman afloat? Well—

For the next several years she continued to be exhibited across the United States. Eventually the *Success* ended up being moored in Sandusky, Ohio.

Then, one night in 1939, she mysteriously sank at her moorings in Sandusky Bay. She was re-floated one last time, cleaned up, and resold.

However, in 1943, while sailing Lake Erie, her new owner accidentally ran her hard aground near Port Clinton. Thinking the cost of salvage too great, the *Success* was abandoned one last time to the elements. Her final sad demise came when local teen-agers burned her once magnificent remains.

The date was July 4, 1946. Ironically, this former *convict ship* met her end on *Independence Day*.

THE FIRST PUBLIC LIBRARY

*T*oo often we take some of the most important things in our lives for granted. So it was for me when thinking of our public libraries.

When I was growing up, I spent hour after hour in our local library. It was a marvelously magical, mystical place that opened up whole new worlds to me. I just imagined libraries had always been there. But, oh no! Originally, only the very rich enjoyed the luxury of having access to books,

All that ended by one man's effort—Benjamin Franklin. He believed knowledge should be available to all the people. So on July 1, 1731, Franklin, along with some of his friends, drew up Articles of Agreement, which created the first public library in this country.

Originally, fifty subscribers put up forty shillings each and promised to pay ten shillings a year to buy books. In addition, many of the original books were donated. They set up shop in Philadelphia, on the corner of Locust and Juniper streets.

The original collection was made up, in part, of about 20 percent literature, 20 percent science, 10 percent philosophy, and only 10 percent theology. This was a far cry from the early libraries of Harvard and Yale where theology prevailed. It would set a precedent for all the libraries that followed.

There was another great distinction. At Franklin's insistence, almost all of the books were only in English, much to the dismay of the scholars of the time. The first two librarians were Ben Franklin and Francis Hopkinson, both of whom went on to sign the Declaration of Independence.

Because cash was scarce in those days, sometimes payment was made with non-monetary items such as stuffed snakes, a set of fossils, a stuffed pelican, and several robes that belonged to Native American chiefs. One person even made payment with an old Revolutionary War sword he dug up in his field. During that war, subscribers were asked to add a bushel of wheat to their annual payment.

Whatever happened to that original library of Benjamin Franklin's creation? Well—

Benjamin Franklin's very first public library has grown to become the oldest, and one of the most prestigious, research libraries in the United States today. It is now called the "Library Company of Philadelphia." It boasts a collection of over 500,000 printed volumes, 75,000 graphics, and 160,000 manuscripts.

What about those early payments which included stuffed animals, artifacts, and even the mummified hand of an Egyptian princess? They all now make up the nucleus of one of the most distinguished collections of early American art and artifacts. The collection documents almost every aspect of American culture, from the colonial times to the nineteenth century.

By the way, the library is still located at 1314 Locust Street in Philadelphia.

THE LOST NOSE

OK! Who did it? *Who did it?* Who stole the nose from the Great Sphinx of Egypt?

Of course, I am speaking of the Great Sphinx monument which still stands at Giza in Egypt. Built around 2500 BC during the reign of Khafre, it has mystified and enthralled mankind for over four-and-a-half millenniums.

It is, indeed, a most imposing structure, rising to a height of sixty-six feet and having a length of 240 feet. It is a stone statue, having the head of a man and the body, legs, and tail of a lion.

The Great Sphinx was supposed to represent the god Horus, who guarded temples and tombs. Its fourteen-foot wide face probably resembled the ruling pharaoh of that time. It soon became a symbol of king-ship. Surrounding this gigantic edifice, many rulers of this period built temples and upright tablets bearing their inscriptions.

ALFY'S AMAZING BUT TRUE

But today, the Great Sphinx has no nose! Where did it go? Many have their theories. Usually these conjectures assume the despots who destroyed this enormous proboscis were military bad guys, making the assumption the nose was intact before their arrival.

To begin, the ancient invasions by Arab conquerors were known to have caused some damage to the Sphinx. An ancient Islamic cleric, Sa'im Al-dahr, left an account of damage he did to this hated symbol.

Another set of culprits were the Mamelukes. They were Turks and Circassians who Genghis Khan sold into slavery to an Egyptian Sultan. Over time they eventually gained control of Egypt. Could they have bumped off the Sphinx's snout for spite?

Recently, Black activist, Louis Farrakhan, while addressing the Million Man March, put forth yet another premise. He suggested, "White supremacy caused Napoleon to blow the nose off the Sphinx because it reminded you too much of the Black man's majesty." There are others who feel Napoleon's troops merely blasted off that magnificent beak for fun in 1798.

British troops, during World War I and II, entered the suspect list. The Brits have been accused of using the Great Sphinx for target practice. During World War II, the Germans also occupied this area and were included in the list of possible nose assassins.

But who did it? Who did away with the Great Sphinx's nose? Well—

Unfortunately, no one really knows for sure.

We know it couldn't have been the British or the Germans during either World War. There is a least one photo dating from 1886 which shows the nose missing. Had Napoleon's troops done the dirty deed, the British would have notified the entire world in a heart beat. No notification was given.

With no solid evidence of the Mamelukes or Arab conquerors doing any nasal mayhem, we are left with only one conclusion: the most probable culprits were time, erosion, and the weather. But no one really knows the entire story of what happened to this mighty nose, except for the Great Sphinx itself, and its not talking.

THE MAN WHO CREATED A
TALKING LEAF

Can you imagine an individual, with no formal education, inventing an entire written language strictly from the riches of his mind? In all of recorded history, it has only happened once. This overlooked genius was a member of the Cherokee Indian Nation.

He was born in 1770. Though his father was a white fur trader, he grew up in his mother's Cherokee village in the territory of Tennessee. His English name was George Guess. But the world would know him as Sequoyah.

As a youth, Sequoyah and his friends witnessed the white men writing messages to one another and reading from books. Most of his friends were convinced that the "talking leaf," as they called it, had been a gift the Great Spirit had inexplicably decided to bestow on the white man, and not the Cherokee people. Sequoyah argued that, far from a gift, it had been created by a human being.

As an adult, Sequoyah became an accomplished silversmith and story teller. But like the rest of his tribe, he was illiterate. As the years passed, the realization that he couldn't read or write haunted him more and more.

When a hunting accident left him with a pronounced limp, he became almost obsessed with the idea of creating a written language. With more leisure time, he spent long periods alone in the woods. Often he appeared to be merely playing with bits of wood. He made strange markings on stones or pieces of birch bark. Unfortunately, he received absolutely no encouragement from his family and friends. At one point, his wife even took all the birch bark, with drawings and symbols he collected over many years, and burned them in the council fire.

When Sequoyah began his quest, he tried to create a different symbol for each word of his language. However, this soon proved impossible. Months soon turned into years. Eventually, after countless experiments, he came to the realization that the Cherokee language was actually composed of a set number of reoccurring sounds.

With this breakthrough, he began to try and identify each of these sounds and assign each sound a symbol.

The learned experts of today will tell you that what he was creating was not an alphabet, but a syllabary.

Finally, in 1821, after twelve long years of trial and error, Sequoyah was ready to introduce his new written language to his nation and the world. Did it work? Was it readily accepted? Well—

To say that the elders of the tribe were skeptical is an understatement. So Sequoyah began by teaching his new written language to his daughter, Ahyoka (A-ga-yuh). When the elders saw how Sequoyah and his daughter were able to communicate complex messages, even when separated a great distance, they were astonished. Some even thought it was magic.

But the only magic in Sequoyah's new written language was its simplicity. Most people who could speak the Cherokee language could learn this new written form in only two or three days. Within a few years, almost the entire Cherokee nation learned to read and write. As for Sequoyah, by the time he died in 1843, he had become an esteemed and respected leader of his nation, all because of his dream to give his people the "talking leaf."

THE MYSTERIOUS COLLYER BROTHERS

*I*t all started at 10:00 a.m. on March 21, 1947. The 122nd Street Police Station in New York City received a call from a Charles Smith saying there was a dead body in a three-story mansion on the corner of Fifth Avenue and 128th Street. The police knew the house well. It had been owned by the Collyer family for almost seventy years.

Originally it housed Dr. Herman Collyer, a wealthy and prominent gynecologist and his musical wife, Susie. They had two sons, Homer and Langley. Both boys were well educated—Homer an engineer and Langley, a lawyer.

But with the divorce and death of their parents, the two brothers slowly became reclusive hermits, never leaving the house. When Homer became blind and paralyzed, brother Langley dedicated his life to providing for his sibling. The only time he was seen was late at night when he foraged out for food and water. He became known as the "ghost man."

Not trusting doctors, Langley decided to cure his brother's blindness. Using his father's 15,000 medical books, he concocted a diet for his ailing brother made up of one hundred oranges a week, black bread, and peanut butter. Believing this would cure the ailing Homer, Langley saved every newspaper, believing his brother would catch up on the news when he recovered his sight.

The last contact anyone had with the reclusive brothers was five years earlier. When they missed a mortgage payment and the bank fail to contact the brothers after numerous attempts, eviction procedures were started. As a work crew arrived to clear the property, Langley screamed at them from an upstairs window to go away.

When police broke down the door and forced their way through wire netting, boxes, barrels, crates, and neck deep debris in the foyer, they found Langley huddled in a clearing that served as the center of his fortress. Quietly, he wrote out a check for $6,700, paying off the mortgage. That was the last time anyone saw either brother alive.

The Collyers had the water, gas, and electricity all turned off. Because of the decay of this area of New York which was known as Harlem, and fearing intruders, they had every entrance barricaded and booby trapped. This made entrance almost impossible.

And what happened when the police did respond to the report of a death at the mansion? Well—

When the police arrived at the Collyer mansion, they found every entrance barricaded and blocked literally with tons of debris. When Patrolman William Barker finally broke through a second story window, he had to tunnel through rubble piled to the ceiling and set with booby traps. Eventually, he found Homer, seated and dressed only in a bathrobe. Homer had apparently died of starvation.

It took over two weeks to find Langley's body. It was only ten feet from his brother, buried under a suitcase, three metal bread boxes, and a huge bundle of newspapers. Langley had apparently been a victim of one of his own booby traps.

In all, over 135 tons of junk was removed from the house, including fourteen grand pianos, a Model T Ford, and human medical specimens, which were preserved in glass jars. The house was condemned and razed. Today the site is a parking lot.

THE PAINTING DIPLOMAT

*P*eter had always been a very independent and intelligent individual. Even as a young man growing up in Antwerp, Belgium in the 1600s, he showed many talents. But he always seemed drawn back to the arts, especially painting.

At the age of twenty-three, he moved to Italy to study art. Soon, he was employed as a painter by the Duke of Mantua. Before long, his reputation as a painter began to spread. Noblemen throughout Europe sought out his talents as an artist. Soon, he had several young artists working as his assistants.

Interestingly, in later life, he was to set aside his work as an artist to enter the world of diplomacy. Peter eventually accepted several diplomatic assignments which involved peace negotiations between Spain and England. He was so successful in his negotiations that King Charles I of England even knighted Peter for his outstanding diplomatic efforts. All of which seemed somewhat ironic, when one looks back on one incident in his life.

At the time, Peter was living in Antwerp, Belgium. During that time, he owned a house that was right next door to a building occupied by the Guild of Archers. A fence had been built between the two buildings, but when it came time for payment of the fence, a dispute arose as to who should pay how much for the fence.

The discussion started to become a bit heated when the Burgomaster of Antwerp, an old acquaintance of Peter's, agreed to act as arbiter. But still the disagreement over the bill for the fence could not be settled.

Finally, the Burgomaster suggested Peter paint a picture for the archers to settle the dispute. Both parties agreed. Before long, Peter completed the painting and presented it to the archers who promptly hung it with pride in the main hall of the Guild of Archers.

So, who was the artist and what was the name of the painting he created? Well—

Are you enough of an art aficionado to have thought of the name of the artist and the painting in question?

The artist was none other than Peter Paul Rubens. And the name of the painting is *Descent from the Cross*, considered by many to be one of the greatest religious paintings of all times. For many years this great masterpiece did, indeed, hang in the main hall of the Guild of Archers.

Today, however, it may be seen on display in the Cathedral of Antwerp. As to its value—it's priceless. But when it was painted, it was done to pay for a fence, because a man, who had been knighted for his diplomacy, could not agree with his neighbor on a debt. What a bargain!

THE REAL BLACK BART

A poetry writing stagecoach robber? That's right! And what's more he called himself Black Bart. But did he really exist? Yes indeed, he did.

It all started on August 3, 1877. A California stagecoach, traveling from Fort Ross to Russian River, was stopped by a lone gunman. He wore a long linen duster and his face was covered by a flour sack, with cut-out holes for the eyes. In a deep voice he said, "Throw down the express box!" The fearful driver quickly complied.

The next day they found that express box. But, in place of the over $600 in coins and checks, there was a poem that read "I've labored long and hard for bread, for honor and for riches; but on my corns too long you've tread, you fine-haired sons of ..." You can probably guess the rest. And it was signed "Black Bart."

Almost a year passed before Black Bart was heard from again. It was on July 25, 1878, that he stopped a stage traveling from Quincy to Oroville, California. Once again he demanded the Wells Fargo box. And this time he made off with over $700 in coins and jewelry.

As before, the box was discovered empty—empty, that is, except for a poem that read "Here I lay me down to sleep, to wait the coming 'morrow; perhaps success, perhaps defeat, and everlasting sorrow. Yet come what will, I'll try it once, my condition can't be worse. And if there's money in that box, 'tis *munny* in my purse."

What made Black Bart's robberies most unique was that he never harmed anyone nor robbed any passenger. He just took the money from the express box, left a note in its place, and then seemed to vanish in thin air.

But his luck started to run out in 1883, when he held up a stage near Copperopolis, California. This time, the express box jammed and cut his hand while he was trying to open it. When another rider arrived, Black Bart scooped up the money and fled, leaving behind a blood soaked handkerchief with the laundry mark "FOX 7". *Was this enough of a clue to catch this poetry writing bandit? Well—*

After checking with ninety-one different laundries, they were finally able to identify the owner of that handkerchief as one Charles E. Bolton. He was a distinguished looking older gentleman, with a gold headed cane and white mustache who was always impeccably dressed in a dapper suit.

In short order, Black Bart, a.k.a. Charles E. Bolton, was tried, convicted, and sentenced to a long term at San Quentin state prison. After just four short years, he was released for "exceptional behavior." Upon leaving prison, he vanished into history, never to be heard from again.

But, Charles E. Bolton left his mark, as Black Bart, the poetry writing, gentleman bandit.

THE REAL CASEY JONES

Mention railroading and you have to mention Casey Jones. Born in 1863, his real name was John Luther Jones. He was described as "…a lovable lad, always in good humor with a big Irish heart, truly loved by all." John Jones got his first railroad job at the age of sixteen. Soon, he was rapidly promoted, first to brakeman and then to fireman. By the age of twenty-six he had already risen to engineer with the Illinois Central Railroad. Because there were several other John Jones on that railroad line, his cohorts renamed him for his hometown, Cayce, Kentucky.

In those days, every kid dreamed of becoming an engineer on an express passenger train. Casey Jones was no exception. Then, in December of 1899, he fulfilled his dream when, at the tender age of thirty-five, he was appointed engineer on the Illinois Central's New Orleans' Special, which ran from Memphis, Tennessee, to Canton, Ohio.

The legend itself actually began just after midnight on April 20, 1900. Train #1, The New Orleans' Special, had just arrived in Memphis—ninety-five minutes late. The engineer for the next leg was supposed to be Sam Tate, but he was sick.

Officially, the company had rules regarding speed. But unofficially, they expected every train to run on time. Any engineer who could accomplish this was regarded as a hero by all.

On this night, Casey and his fireman, Sim Webb, were asked to take the run to Canton, even though they had both just completed eleven hours on duty. Though nothing was said, everyone knew there was no one who could get more speed out of a steam engine than Casey Jones.

He had to make up ninety-five minutes in just 188 miles while passing six trains. This had to be accomplished on a single track with only two places to pass. Confident as ever, Casey and Sim set out— throttle wide open.

Less than four hours later, at the Vaughan Siding, four trains were trying to saw past one another. Sawing was a maneuver of moving trains back and forth from the main line to the siding to try and make room for Old Number One. They were confident that they had plenty of time. They didn't know Casey Jones was at the throttle.

Suddenly, seemingly from out of nowhere, Old Number One came screaming around a blind corner. Hearing the warning torpedoes which had been placed on the tracks by the switchman from the trains ahead, Casey yelled at his fireman to jump. Then, with one hand on the air brake and the other on his beloved whistle, he rode Old Number One to his death as it crashed into that switching freight.

And what was the aftermath? Well—

In the end, Superintendent Sullivan, who filed the official report, concluded that "Engineer Jones was solely responsible." The report continued, "The actual damage of this collision amount to be paid is—$3,323.75."

Though Casey Jones was the only fatality, four other people received the following settlements: Fireman Sim Webb, for body bruises, $5; passenger

William Miller, slight injuries, $25; two postal clerks who were jarred, $1 each.

And it might have ended there had it not been for one Wallace Sanders, an illiterate engine wiper, who composed the original "Ballad of Casey Jones" which eventually swept the nation. And so Casey Jones entered into our folklore to live on in the hearts and minds of Americans.

THE REAL DAVY CROCKETT

*H*aving taught American history, I know how hard it is for any historian at times to separate fact from fiction. This is especially true in the case of our quintessential American hero, Davy Crockett.

In the case of Mr. Crockett, the problem lies in the fact that much of our information about this American icon comes from his autobiography. Not actually an autobiography, per se, these writings consisted of a series of Crockett almanacs which Davy helped write.

To begin with, most historians agree Crockett was born in 1786 in eastern Tennessee. According to legend, he "...killed him a b'ar when he was only three." But at least one reliable source states that his parents still had young Davy in dresses at that age.

It was Crockett who proclaimed himself "King of the Wild Frontier." However, as one reporter stated,

"He was never king of anything, except maybe the Tennessee tall tales and bourbon sampler's association." In one of his writings, Davy contended he shot 105 bears in only nine months. His drinking companion, however, discounted this on the grounds that Crockett couldn't count that high.

Legend presented our frontiersman as such a great Indian fighter that when Walt Disney unveiled its mini-series about Crockett, the first episode was entitled, "Davy Crockett, Indian Fighter." Alas, in truth, at least once Crockett was reported to have hired a substitute to go fight in those wars for him.

He did seem to stay with his first wife until her death in 1815. As for the second wife, he left her, broke, with children from their marriage *and* two boys from his first marriage.

Much is made of the four years he spent in the Tennessee state legislature and the six years he served in the United States Congress. This was, indeed, quite a feat for someone with less than six months of schooling. However, what usually isn't mentioned is the fact that he had one of the worst attendance records in the entire history of the Congress.

And finally, Crockett died at the Alamo. Now that is true. But was he the last to die on that heroic battle, blazing pistol in one hand, a flailing sword in the other, and screaming "Long live Texas" with his dying breathe, as legend would have it? What is fact and what is fiction? Well—

Now, everyone agrees that Davy Crockett did, indeed, die at the Alamo. However, beyond this point stories begin to differ.

The official account tells how he left success behind to go and fight on for right and justice. Then there is another account that relates how, angered by his defeat in the Congress, Davy told his constituents to go to Hades. Leaving his wife and kids behind, he set out with twelve men for adventure in Texas. There is little doubt that he must have raised the morale of the embattled troops in the Alamo with his tall tales and fiddle playing.

Of course, the movies never actually showed him dying, but the official report had him falling toward the end of the battle near the chapel wall. Recently discovered accounts now indicate that Crockett probably survived the battle, only to be executed with five other survivors by the direct order of General Santa Anna.

THE SECRET OF THE
KING JAMES BIBLE

*T*hroughout literary history, few books of spiritual inspiration have garnered higher praise for poetic beauty than the four-hundred-year-old King James' version of the Bible. And yet, despite its great acclaim, we have no idea who actually translated this masterpiece. But maybe, just maybe, we might be able to find a clue.

First, let's go back to the beginning. The year was 1610. Up until this time, if any individual wanted to read the Bible, they would have had to know Greek, Hebrew, or Latin. The church declared that only *men* of God should be allowed to read and interpret this most holy of books. If anyone tried to translate the Bible into English, all copies would have been confiscated and burned. Then, the author would be convicted of heresy and burned alive at the stake.

In 1603, King James ascended the throne of England and became not only its king, but also the head of the Church of England. By 1604, King James decided he wanted an English translation of the Bible. At this time in England, great writers were in abundance. Even the immortal William Shakespeare would have been available for this most important of tasks. King James had the best from which to choose.

And soon, the great task of translating the Bible into English was begun. Yet, throughout it all, no one was allowed to be identified with its authorship. To this day, there is no evidence of exactly who translated any part of the King James Version of the Bible—or is there? Could it be that one small hint of authorship of this magnificent work has survived the centuries? Well—

To begin with, it is important to remember the bulk of the translation of the King James Version of the Bible was completed in 1610. In 1610 William Shakespeare would have been forty-six years old. Remember, William Shakespeare was forty-six years old when most of this translation occurred.

To find our clue we must go to the forty-sixth book of Psalms in the King James Version of the Bible.

Start counting each word from the beginning of the forty-sixth book of Psalms until you find the forty-sixth word from the beginning. Now go to the end of the forty-sixth Psalm. Exclude the last word, "Selah." It merely means "The end, so be it." Most scholars agree it was added by an editor much later. Not including "Selah," count every word until you find the forty-sixth word from the end of this Psalm.

If you have counted correctly, you will find that the forty-sixth word from the beginning is "shake" and the forty-sixth word from the end is "spear," in the forty-sixth Psalm which was written in the forty-sixth year of William Shakespeare's life.

Does this mean William Shakespeare wrote this part of the King James Version of the Bible? I'll leave that answer to far greater scholars than me. I would like to know what you think.

THE STORY OF TAPS

*T*he following story came to me from an article written by Lt. Colonel Lewis Kirkpatrick for *The Officer Magazine*, May of 1998 issue.

This story begins in 1862, near the beginning of the Civil War. A unit of union soldiers encamped near Harrisson's Landing in Virginia was commanded by Captain Robert Ellicombe. Just beyond a narrow parcel of land was the Confederate army.

Throughout that long night, Captain Ellicombe heard the moan of a soldier who had been mortally wounded earlier that day and still lay on the battlefield. Unaware of whether it was a Union or Confederate recruit, the captain decided, at the risk of his own life, to bring the wounded soldier back for medical aid. Under constant gunfire, the captain crawled forward until he reached the moaning, wounded soldier. Ever so slowly, he began inching him back toward the union lines.

It wasn't until the captain reached the security of his own troops that he finally realized that this was a confederate soldier, and he was already dead. It was then that the captain lit a torch. Suddenly, he gasped with horror. There, in that dim torch light, shined the face of the soldier. There was no mistaking it. The face of the dead soldier he had risked his life to rescue turned out to be his only son. Before the war, the boy decided to study music in the South. Without saying a word to his father, he joined the confederate forces.

The next morning, the heart-broken father asked his superiors for permission to give his son a full military funeral. As part of the request, the father asked that an army band play a funeral dirge for his son's burial service. His superiors denied that request, since his son was a confederate soldier. However, the father was granted one musician, a bugler.

The father found a series of musical notes on a piece of paper in his son's uniform. He asked for the bugler to play the tune. His superior granted this request.

And what was the melody that drifted out that night over his son's grave? Well—

You probably would recognize both the tune and the words that were added later, "Day is done, gone the sun, from the lakes, from the hills, from the sky. All is well, safely rest, God is nigh."

Yes, it was "Taps," the only, truly American bugle call. Is this story true? I don't know. But I hope so. And maybe, just maybe, on that battlefield almost a century and a half ago, as Captain Ellicombe sat listening to that tune drift out over his son's grave, he was thinking the same indelible words that were penned almost one hundred years later by playwright Arthur Miller, "THEY ARE ALL MY SONS!"

THE STRANGE DEMISE OF
MICHAEL MALLOY

Michael Malloy, an Irish immigrant, was a sixty-year-old unemployed fireman, and a legendary drinker in the Bronx, New York. When his bar tab at Tony Marino's speakeasy got too high in January of 1933, Malloy was finally cut off. But Malloy continued coming around, mooching drinks.

Times were hard for bar owner Marino. Then one day, another patron, an undertaker by the name of Francis Pasqua, got an idea. About a year before, Marino and Pasqua had conspired with three other friends. Together, they took out an $800 life insurance policy on Marino's girl friend. With the policy in force, they got the lady in question drunk and laid her, passed out, on her own bed. They then doused her with water and open the windows of her room to the cold winter night's air. The next morning she was discovered, dead, and they promptly collected their $800. Why not do a repeat with Michael Malloy?

They agreed, and the "murder trust," as the papers later dubbed them, went into action. They took out three separate policies on Malloy's life. Marino was named beneficiary on all three policies. Malloy was then put back on an unlimited tab. It was the consensus of all concerned that he would soon drink himself to death. But Malloy just kept coming in for more!

They then resolved to spike his drinks with poisonous antifreeze. But each day he would show up refreshed and thirsty as ever. Undaunted, they began to add turpentine, horse liniment, and even rat poison to his daily brew. But alcoholic Malloy not only tolerated these concoctions, he seemed to enjoy the new flavors.

Relentless, our merry band of five decided to serve up Malloy a batch of spoiled oysters which had been soaked in wood alcohol. They followed up the very next day with a feast of canned sardines, which had been opened and spoiled for a week. To give it zest, they added the ground up can and some chopped up pins. Malloy thought it was delicious.

Getting impatient, they got him so drunk he passed out. They then laid him out in Clairmount

Park in fourteen degree weather, soaked him with water, and left him to freeze. The next day he came into the bar and complained of a slight chill.

In desperation, they got Malloy drunk one last time, ran him over with a car, and left him, surely to die. Then they waited—and waited—but no obituaries appeared. They checked the hospitals—nothing!

Totally exasperated they decided to substitute another derelict, Joseph Patrick Murray. They got him drunk, placed Malloy's identification on him, and ran him over—not once, but twice!

And did they succeed? Well—

Unbelievably, no! Miraculously, Joseph Patrick Murray survived. And to add insult to injury, three weeks later Michael Malloy strolled into the speakeasy, thirsty as ever.

That did it. Our merry band of murderers started serving Malloy wood alcohol until he passed out. Then they took him to Murphy's apartment, connected a hose from the stove to Malloy's mouth, and turned on the gas. They finally succeeded. On February 22, 1933, they killed Michael Malloy.

But as you can imagine, even this didn't work out as planned. Word soon leaked out and within two weeks arrests were made of the five in the "murder trust." One went to jail, while Tony Marino and the other three kept a date with the electric chair at Sing Sing prison.

And is this story true? According to the *New York Times*, oh yes! Besides, who could have made it up?

THE VOLCANO AND
THE POLITICIAN

*I*n recent times, I began to think there are a few politicians today who would do anything to win an election. Then I read about Mouttet from Martinique, a French controlled island in the West Indies.

It was May of 1912. Recently appointed governor Mouttet was in charge of overseeing the upcoming elections in St. Pierre. The race was between the established white supremacy party and the radical party made up of Martinique's black and mulatto majority. It was literally white against black, rich against poor.

Things were heating up, not only in the political arena, but also in the giant volcano on nearby Mount Pelee. In April, for the first time since 1851, Mount Pelee's volcano started to rumble with a vengeance, spewing ash and noxious fumes throughout the narrow streets of St. Pierre.

Governor Mouttet was concerned that an evacuation would effect the May tenth elections, as the only ones who could afford to leave town would be the affluent whites.

With this in mind, he persuaded the island's largest newspaper, *Les Colonies*, to downplay the danger from the volcano. The paper, a supporter of Governor Mouttet, feared a loss of advertising revenue if the radical party won. In bold headlines the paper reported the ever growing fear and panic over Mount Pelee's activity was actually a conspiracy of the radical party. A telegram from the American consul to Washington was even intercepted and changed to state the eruption was subsiding and the danger gone. This was not true.

As ash from the volcano continued to rain down, hundreds fled the countryside to find refuge in St. Pierre, swelling the population to well over 30,000. On the evening of May seventh, the governor and his wife arrived in town to restore the confidence of the people. Almost immediately he realized the gravity of the situation. He planned to announce the evacuation of the town at high mass at the cathedral the next day. Mouttet never got to make the announcement.

At 7:59 a.m. the following morning, the volcano on Mount Pelee erupted, with an avalanche of lava and fumes that had temperatures exceeding 1,300 degrees. This torrent from hell moved at speeds of over sixty miles an hour.

Did anyone in St. Pierre survive this earth shattering eruption? Well—

On that very day, almost in the blink of an eye, 30,000 people lost their lives, including the governor and his wife. The temperature was so intense most people had their clothes seared from their bodies.

When the smoke cleared, only two survivors could be found. One was a twenty-eight-year-old cobbler who lived on the outskirts of town. Prior to the eruption, his house had been so inundated by refugees that he was forced to take refuge in his basement and was spared.

The only other survivor was a nineteen-year-old black convict who was found in the rubble of his own cell. Ironically, he had been sentenced to hang that very afternoon for murder, but survived. And the 30,000 citizens of St. Pierre, including the governor who had sentenced him, perished.

THE WORLD'S FIRST BULL DOGGER

*N*o sporting activity can be considered more all-American than the rodeo. For over a century, American cowboys and cowgirls have entertained and thrilled spectators all over the world.

The rodeo was actually developed out of the cattle drives that took place in the western parts of this country during the latter half of the nineteenth century. Whenever two different cattle outfits met on the trail, inevitably, the cowboys took some time out to compete in bronco riding and steer roping just to see who could lay claim to bragging rights. Legend has it that the first rodeo for spectators took place in Pecos, Texas, in 1883.

If you go to a modern day rodeo, all of the events you watch actually evolved out of the day-to-day skills needed by a cowboy in the old West—all, that is, except one: bulldogging or steer wrestling.

History tells us this exciting form of competition was actually invented by one individual cowboy. His name was Bill Pickett. He was more popularly known as the Dusky Demon. Pickett would tell anyone who listened that there wasn't a bull alive anywhere on earth that he couldn't stay with for five minutes. During his career he was reputed to have wrestled over five thousand different steers, including Mexican bulls, Scottish Highland steers, and almost every other breed imaginable.

Pickett had a most unique technique for dominating these massive animals. He would bring them all down and then proceed to hold them down—by biting on their upper lips. And it really worked. A similar version of this same technique, called twitching, is still used today to handle horses while shoeing or medicating them. Instead of biting their upper lip, a small chain is put around the lip and twisted just tight enough to distract the animal.

But, whatever happened to this historic cowboy who is credited with inventing bulldogging? Well—

As for Bill Pickett, he went on to perform his very "special talent" for rodeos around the world, being seen by millions. He even had Will Rogers as a best friend.

After his death, he probably would have faded into obscurity had it not been for the United States

Postal Service. In 1993, they mistakenly released a Bill Pickett commemorative stamp—with someone else's picture on it. When the postal service corrected the mistake by issuing a new stamp, it turned the world's first bull dogger into a legend.

Bill Pickett, the man who invented bull dogging, and oh, yes, I might add, Bill Pickett, African-American, was, indeed, one of the greatest American cowboys of all time.

THEY TAMED THE WEST

*T*heir contribution to the opening of America's frontier is unquestioned. They were called The Buffalo Soldiers.

On July 28, 1866, an Act of Congress "…to increase and fix the military peace establishment…" created four new regiments of cavalry within the armed forces of the United States. Two of these regiments were to be "composed of colored men." They were designated the Ninth and Tenth Cavalry.

Within a year, they would help to open a new chapter in the history of the American West. Theirs would be the thankless task of dealing with many of the Indian wars in the West.

No one really knows the origin of the name Buffalo Soldiers. Some feel it was a term of respect paid to them by the Indians of the plains who saw the buffalo as a sacred animal.

When the word went out that these units were being organized, large numbers of men showed up to volunteer for the five-year enlistment period. Most, however, were turned down because they were too young, too old, or physically unfit. It seems the wretched food and squalid living conditions provided by the slave owners had taken their toll.

Those who were accepted were given $13 a month, quarters, meals, and uniforms. Veterans of the Civil War were appointed corporals and sergeants. However, the biggest inducement for enlisting was the prospect of learning to read and write. Prior to Lincoln, African-Americans, by law, were denied an education.

Their lot would not be an easy one. The food was monotonous: boiled beef, hash, beans, bread, and occasionally a cup of coffee. Black cavalry men were routinely thrown out of barrooms and beaten in the streets. They received the most wretched horses in the country. But worst of all they received no respect.

However, this was not always the case. A few officers were different. It was Colonel Benjamin Garrison who ordered that they never be called "colored," but simply the Tenth Regiment—period. With this support the Buffalo Soldiers went on to serve with valor while trying to deal with the violence of the turbulent West.

By the time of the Apaches' final surrender, the Buffalo Soldiers had distinguished themselves as two of the best fighting units in the United States Army. In all, they earned twelve Congressional Medals of Honor.

But were officers eager to command the Ninth and Tenth Regiments? Well—

Sadly, the answer was usually, no. Even with the promise of greater rank and fast promotion, most officers felt commanding the Ninth and Tenth Cavalry Units was a dead end assignment.

This was especially true of one officer. This particular officer graduated from West Point at the bottom of his class, with a record number of demerits. He did, however, gain recognition and the rank of general during the Civil War, despite a record number of casualties to his unit.

With the war ended, he was demoted to Lt. Colonel. Hoping for glory, promotion, and perhaps even a run at the presidency, Lt. Colonel George Armstrong Custer flatly refused command of the Buffalo Soldiers. Instead, he was assigned to the Seventh Cavalry and went off to meet his fate at Little Big Horn. He never did make general or become president.

TRADITION, HONOR, PATRIOTISM

*T*radition, honor, patriotism! These are words that have been emblazoned in the hearts of mankind since time immortal. Yet, how many individuals are ever called upon to make major sacrifices in their lives in order to live up to these three simple words? One man truly did. His name was Lieutenant Hiroo Onoda, the last Japanese soldier to surrender from World War II.

Born in 1922, Hiroo was drafted into the Japanese army in May 1942. After limited action in China, he was selected for officer school, and then sent on for secret intelligence training.

Upon completion of all his training, Hiroo was sent to the small Philippine island of Lubang to gather intelligence and direct guerrilla warfare. His orders, as he later recounted in his autobiography, were "You are absolutely forbidden to die by your own hand. It may take years, but whatever happens, we'll come back for you. You may have to live on coconuts, but under no circumstances are you to give up your life voluntarily."

But the end was near for Japan. Soon, the American troops swept over the island. Eventually, there were only four Japanese soldiers left alive in the thick mountainous terrain: Onoda, Kosuka, Shimada, and Akatsu.

In August 1945, leaflets were dropped throughout the island stating, "The war ended on August fifteenth, come down from the mountains." But the four warriors vowed to keep fighting.

Then, in September 1949, Akatsu deserted. Six months later Onoda found a note from Akatsu saying the Philippine soldiers had treated him like a friend. But the three fought on.

In 1952, a plane dropped copies of letters and photos from their friends and relatives, begging them to surrender. They, however, doubted their authenticity. As time passed, Shimada grew despondent, missing his wife and children. In May 1954, when shots were exchanged with an island search party, Onoda and Kozuka dove for cover. Shimada, however, stood tall, aimed his gun, but never fired. He was killed with a single bullet.

Now only Onoda and Kozula were left. As years passed into decades, they perfected their survival skills. To mend their only suit of clothes, they made needles from wire and thread from the hemp-like jungle plants. They lived primarily on bananas and coconut milk. For security, they always slept with their clothes on. Then, during a raid on a nearby rice field in 1972, Kozuka was killed.

But what finally happened to Onoda, Japan's last soldier from World War II? Well—

In 1973, after a failed search party left, Onoda found a poem that read, "Not even an echo responds to my call in the summery mountains." It had been written by his aged father who was with the search party.

Finally, in 1974, a Japanese student, conducting his own search, made contact with this last warrior. Onoda told him that he would only surrender if ordered to by his superior officer, Major Taniguchi. After an exhaustive search, remarkably, the major was found. Returning to Onoda, he relieved his last warrior of command. Onoda's thirty-year war was finally over.

After writing his memoirs, *No Surrender: My 30-Year War*, Hiroo Onoda retired to Brazil to live out his life in solitude on his 2,800-acre cattle ranch.

WAS KILROY REALLY HERE?

*I*t was undoubtedly the most well-known piece of graffiti ever to occur in the twentieth century. Who hasn't seen the phrase, "Kilroy was here?" But who was Kilroy?

To the GI's during World War II, it became the symbol of the super American GI who always got there first. The challenge was to write "Kilroy was here" in the most unlikely places. Legend has it that it has been scrawled atop Mt. Everest, the Statue of Liberty, the underside of the Arch de Triumph, and even spelled out in the dust of the moon.

In 1945, an outdoor toilet was constructed at the site of the Potsdam Conference. It was for the exclusive use of Roosevelt, Stalin, and Churchill. The first to use it was Stalin. When he came out, he was reported to have asked his aide in Russian, "Who is this Kilroy?"

Kilroy even made it to the Pacific. When the underwater demolition divers swam ashore on Japanese held islands to prepare the beaches for the upcoming landings of U.S. troops, they were certain they were the first GIs to arrive. Wrong! Time after time they reported seeing "Kilroy was here" scrawled all over. Once they even reported seeing the enemy painting over this logo which had been placed there before the arrival of the Americans or Japanese. And when they didn't find any Kilroy logo, they made sure they left one for others to find.

But where or how did this phenomenon start? Was there a real Kilroy? Yes, indeed. His name was James J. Kilroy, from Halifax, Massachusetts. He worked in the Fore River shipyard where his job was to check and count all the rivets made on the new ships. Accuracy was important because the riveters got paid by the number of rivets placed.

To mark the spot he ended his count, Kilroy would place an "X" on the bulkhead. But often the riveters would erase the "X" after he left so that the next checker would count the rivets twice, thus making them more money.

When Kilroy found this out, he scrawled "Kilroy was here," in huge letters next to his "X." Often these troop ships would be sent out before this could be painted over. Soon, the GIs aboard these ships picked up on the mysterious scrawl, and it was spread to the four corners of the earth. The tradition carried on for decades to come, even throughout the Vietnam War.

But, how was the original Kilroy finally discovered. Well—

It happened in December in the late 1940s. All of the radio stations were announcing that a wonderful prize would be given to anyone who could prove they started the "Kilroy was here" fad.

Hearing this, James and Margaret Kilroy decided to step forth. Having nine children to provide Christmas presents for, they needed all the help they could get. They brought forth riveters, managers, and supervisors who verified the Kilroy story.

The prize, provided by the sponsoring Transit Company of America, was a real, honest-to-goodness, two-ton trolley. Much to the joy of the Kilroy children, it was standing in their yard on Christmas morning. And scrawled on the ceiling of the trolley were the words "Santa was here."

WHO WAS "UNCLE SAM"?

*P*ut on your red, white, and blue, 'cause it's time for a story of real patriotism, the origin of Uncle Sam.

His likeness is seen everywhere, walking on ten-foot stilts in parades, recruiting for the military, or hawking some product on television. But where did our beloved Uncle Sam come from? Who originated him?

Although some disagree, the most popular explanation is that Uncle Sam was actually modeled after a real person. His name was Samuel Wilson. He was born in Massachusetts on September 13, 1766.

While a youth, he played with another American icon, John Chapman, later to be known as Johnny Appleseed. At the age of fourteen, Samuel fought in the American Revolutionary War. Reaching manhood, he moved to Troy, New York, and opened a meat-packing company. Wilson soon gained the name Uncle Sam because of his smiley demeanor and fair business practices.

When the War of 1812 broke out, Sam procured a contract to provide beef and pork for the soldiers stationed at Troy. To indicate that certain shipments were destined for military use only, Wilson would stamp the crates "U.S." for United States, even though this abbreviation was not yet being used.

Then one day, October 1, 1812, a government inspector asked what the initials stood for. A nearby worker jokingly replied, "That means it comes from our Uncle Sam." The term caught on. Soon all government rations and supplies were said to be the property of Uncle Sam. Even the soldiers called themselves Uncle Sam's men.

By 1820, illustrations of Uncle Sam began to appear in New England newspapers, showing him in a black top hat and a black tailcoat. During President Jackson's administration, Uncle Sam's pants became red. It was Abraham Lincoln who inspired the addition of a beard.

By the end of the nineteenth century, he had grown to national prominence, wearing red pants with white stripes and a top hat with both stars and stripes. Famed cartoonist Thomas Nast made him tall, thin, and with hollow cheeks, resembling the real life Samuel Wilson. But it was James Montgomery Flagg who finished the portrait for a July 6, 1916, cover of *Leslie's Weekly*. And is this story true? Well—

To this day there are those who dispute it.

However, in 1961, historian Thomas Gerson found a May 12, 1830, issue of the *New York Gazette* newspaper. It told how one Pheodorus Bailey, postmaster of New York, while a soldier, accompanied government inspectors on that fateful day in October of 1812 and heard the worker surmise that the stamped initials "U.S." stood for his boss, Uncle Sam Wilson. Whereupon, the Congress of the United States officially proclaimed Samuel Wilson to be the original Uncle Sam. To this day, Samuel Wilson's gravesite at Oakwood Cemetery in Troy, New York is lovingly cared for by the local Boy Scouts.

Yes, there are still those who question whether Sam Wilson was the original inspiration for Uncle Sam. But as for me, I am not about to argue with the Congress of these United States *and* the Boy Scouts of America.

WILL ROGERS' DISCOVERY

*I*n the history of this country, few, if any, entertainers were more beloved than the legendary
Will Rogers. This pride of America was known the
world around for his caring, friendly ways. He truly
tried to live up to his credo, "I never met a man I
didn't like."

Never was his open friendliness more apparent
than on the night he strolled into a telegraph office
in a small town in his home state of Oklahoma.
While waiting for his message to be sent, he struck up
a conversation with the youthful telegraph operator.
Recognizing the great Will Rogers, the young man
was almost speechless.

Before long, Rogers noticed a guitar propped up
in the corner of the telegraph office. He asked the
young man if the guitar belonged to him. With a shy
grin, the youth admitted ownership. The lad then

went on to confess, with some embarrassment, that because of his love for music, he had squandered the first $1.50 he had ever earned on the purchase of that instrument. With an eager grin, Rogers prevailed upon the young man to strike up a tune. The young operator chose a familiar ballad and gave it his best.

From the opening refrain, Will Rogers was enthralled. After an encore, Rogers bid the youthful troubadour farewell and started to leave. Then, he turned back to the budding songster and told him he was very impressed with his talent. Rogers went on to strongly encourage him to go into show business. With that, the great Will Rogers turned and disappeared in the night with the joyful voice of that young telegraph operator still singing in his heart.

Will Rogers, of course, went on to entertain his loving audiences until his death in a plane crash in 1935 which saddened an entire nation. And what ever happened to that youthful, singing telegraph operator? Well—

Any ideas as to the identity of that young singing telegraph operator? Here are some clues.

As you have probably guessed by now, the young man did, indeed, decide to go into entertainment. And oh, how he entertained us! He went on to become one of America's most beloved cowboys in the movies, on radio, and even on television. His recording of "Rudolph, the Red Nose Reindeer" became one of the biggest selling Christmas records ever. He even became the owner and number one fan of the California Angels baseball team.

You are right. It was none other than Gene Autry who entertained Will Rogers on that warm summer night in a telegraph office in a small town in Oklahoma.

WINNING THE LOTTERY

What's a person have to do to get rich? Aha! Go and get yourself a winning lottery ticket. It seems to have become a national pastime. But where did the lottery originate?

Remarkably, we can trace it all the way back to Moses. It was in the Bible's book of Numbers. There Moses used a lottery to award land west of the Jordan River. The Romans seem to be the next to get into the act, setting up lotteries about 2,000 years ago. It was the Chinese, during the Hun Dynasty, who invented Keno and used it to help fund the building of the Great Wall of China.

One of the first recorded lotteries run by an individual was the widow of the great Flemish painter, Jan Van Eyck, who raffled off his remaining paintings in 1446. Within twenty years, Belgium was using lotteries to pay for the building of chapels, poorhouses, canals, and ports.

It was Genoa, Italy, in 1515, that used a lottery to select members of their senate. As a matter of fact, the word *lottery* is derived from the Italian word *lotto* which means "destiny" or "fate."

Soon, Queen Elizabeth of England got into the lottery game, with prizes which included cash, china, and tapestries. Then in 1612, her successor, King James I, by royal decree, established a game of chance to help finance the first British colony in America—Jamestown, Virginia.

Of course, it didn't take long for the American colonies to catch on. And who suggested it? Why, Benjamin Franklin, of course. He suggested the use of lotteries to pay for cannons to fight the British during the Revolutionary War. George Washington used a sweepstake to pay for the building of the mountain road which opened westward expansion from Virginia.

During the early 1800s, fifty colleges, three hundred schools, and two hundred churches were erected from lottery profits. These included such notable names as Columbia, Yale, Princeton, and even Harvard.

But then the tide began to turn. By 1878, every state except Louisiana had banned lotteries. By 1905, all lotteries in this country were effectively shut down for the next sixty years. During the thirties, forties, and fifties, the only legal lottery Americans had to turn to was the infamous "Irish Sweepstakes."

Finally, in 1964, New Hampshire reopened the door by tying a new lottery to horse racing. But, what are one's odds of winning a lottery? Well—

First, let's put it in perspective by looking at some other odds in life. To begin with, the chances of collecting on a term life insurance policy in force are 1 in 35. Your odds of getting audited by the IRS: 1 in 75. How about your odds of losing your luggage on an airplane flight in the U.S.? 1 in 250. Your odds of getting murdered are about 1 in 12,000.

What are the chances of four PGA golfers all getting a hole-in-one on the same hole? 1 in 332,000. The odds of your getting struck by lightning: 1 in 400,000.

And finally, what are the odds of your winning the top prize in the multi-state Power Ball lottery? 1 in 120,526,770. *That's three hundred times the chance of getting struck by lightning.* Good luck!

INVITATION

We are losing history every day because some-one fails to record it. History is all around us. It was our ancestors, yours and mine, who lived what we now call history. With this in mind, we have established the "Tales of American History Preservation Society," or TAHPS. We are looking for those "Amazing, But True" stories which may come from *your* ancestors or *your* family past for our next volume of "Alfy's Amazing But True…"

We would like you to be part of TAHPS. You are invited to help in our ongoing effort to preserve our history. If you have a true story from history you would like to have preserved for posterity, please forward it to Alfy's Books, 2527 Charles St. N., North Saint Paul, Minnesota 55109. Be certain to include any and all documentation for the story. All stories should be about 450-600 words in length. If your story is used in our next volume, you will be credited with authorship and you will receive a financial stipend.

We would love to hear from you. Be part of TAHPS and help preserve our history!

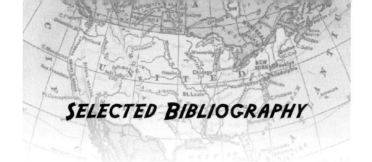

SELECTED BIBLIOGRAPHY

Books

Asimov, Isaac. *Book of Facts*. New York: Wings Books, 1979.

At the Instance of Benjamin Franklin. Philadelphia: The Library Company of Philadelphia, 1995.

Barnes, Harry Elmer. *An Intellectual and Cultural History of the Western World, Volumes 1, 2, 3*. New York City: Dover Publications, Inc., 1965.

Bathroom Readers Institute. *Uncle John's Bathroom Readers. Series 1-4*. Berkeley: St. Martins Press, 1988-1991.

Discovering Historic Iowa Transportation Milestones, Ames, Iowa: Iowa Department of Transportation, 2000.

Hix, Elsie. *Strange as It Seems*. New York City: Bantam Books, 1960.

Kane, Joseph Nathan. *Facts About the Presidents*. New York City: The Pocket Books, 1960.

Olds, Elizabeth Fagg. *Women of the Four Winds*. Boston: Houghton Mifflin Company, 1985.

Ripley's Believe It or Not! 2nd Series. New York City: The Pocket Books, 1948.

Ripley's Believe It or Not! 4th Series. New York City: The Pocket Books, 1957.

Ripley's Believe It or Not! 14th Series. New York City: The Pocket Books, 1968.

Roberts, Nancy. *Blackbeard and Other Pirates of the Atlantic Coast*. Winston-Salem, N. C.: John F. Blair, 1993.

The Bible, King James Version

Thomas, Robert D. *The Old Farmers 2001 Almanac*. Dublin, New Hampshire: Yankee Publishing, Inc., 2000.

Tuleja, Tad. *Fabulous Fallacies*. New York City: Galahad Books, 1982.

Wallechinsky, David and Irving Wallace. *The People's Almanac:* Garden City, New Jersey: Doubleday & Company, 1975.

Wallechinsky, David and Irving Wallace. *The People's Almanac # 2*. New York City: William Morrow & Company, 1978.

Wicks, Hamilton S. *Chronicles of Oklahoma*. Oklahoma City: Oklahoma Historical Society Press, June 1926.

Letters

Beckett, Gary. Director, Corporate Communications, Outboard Marine Corporation. To Alfred A. E. Wolfram, January 24, 2000.

Craig, Park Ranger Joe, Saratoga National Historical Park. To Alfred A. E. Wolfram, March 10, 2000.

Sullivan, A, W., General Superintendent, Illinois Central Railroad. To J. T. Jaraham, 2nd Vice President, Illinois Central Railroad, April 30, 1900.

Magazines

Hansen, Peter A. "The Brave Engineer" *Trains*. Volume 60, Number 4, April 2000, page 34.

Kirkpatrick, Lt. Colonel Lewis. "The Story of Taps" *The Officer*. May 1998.

Newspapers

"An Easter Calm." *St. Louis Republican*, April 22, 1889, page 1.

New York Times, May 13, 1933, page 28, column 2; May 26, 1933, page 27, column 3; May 26, 1933, page 7, column 1; October 8, 1933, page 44, column 3; October 20, 1933, page 38, column 2; June 8, 1934, page 44, column 4; June 20, 1934, page 4, column 7; July 6, 1934, page 10, column 2.

New York Herald, May 13, 1933, page 26, column 4; May 17, 1933, page 36, column 4; May 26, 1933, page 3, column 5; October 1, 1933, page 3, column 2; October 12, 1933, page 3, column 6; October 14, 1933, page 3, column 6; October 18, 1933, age 3, column 1; October 20, 1933, page 3, column 1; October 21, 1933, page 3, column 4.

"On to Oklahoma." *Kansas City Star*. March 22, 1924, page 3.

Pamphlets

African American Oklahomans. Oklahoma City: Oklahoma Historical Society, 1998.

America's Oldest Cultural Institution. Philadelphia: The Library Company of Philadelphia, 2000.

The Buffalo Soldiers. Oklahoma City: Oklahoma Historical Society, 1998.

Guide to Numbers Games. Roseville, Minnesota: Minnesota State Lottery, 1999.

Sequoyah's Home Site. Oklahoma City: Oklahoma Historical Society, 1999.

A *Short History of Oklahoma*. Oklahoma City: Oklahoma Historical Society, 1999.

Plays

Wolfram, Alfred A. E., *An American Odyssey.* Winona, Minnesota, 2003.

Wolfram, Alfred A. E., *The Shakespeare Man*. Blaine, Minnesota, 1992.

Radio

Adams, Noah and Mara Liasson. *All Things Considered*, National Public Radio, January 27, 2000.

Web Sites

Americanhistory.about.com

americanwest.com

arab.net/Egypt/tour

danger-ahead.railfan.net

earth.nwu.edu

encyclopedia.com

fermi.bed.ushicago.edu

gaytoday.badpuppy.com

geocities.com

home.nycap.it.com

kilroy.com

library.saratoga.ny.us

msc.cornell.edu

naspl.org

napul@mail.elender.hu

nydailynews.com

ourworld.compuserve.com

sandiegohistory.org

transhistory.org

ucla.edu

undelete.org

webleyweb.com

whitehouse.gov

wtvh.com

xroads.virginia.edu

yoyo.cc.monash.edu

Cleaver Hoaxs

Public Library of Mt. Vernon and Knox County
Sulabh International Museum of Toilets

Special Thanks

Joe Craig, Park Ranger, Saratoga National Historical Park
Max Nichols, Oklahoma Historical Society
National Maritime Museum, Pymont, New South Wales, Australia

ABOUT THE AUTHOR

A true renaissance man, Alfred A. E. Wolfram is a successful writer, actor/performer, speaker/educator, business executive, and accomplished blue-water sailor.

Having written for newspapers and magazines, Mr. Wolfram had his own column which appeared in numerous Minnesota newspapers and also wrote a course study for teaching theatre in Iowa schools.

For over four decades he has entertained and informed audiences far and wide, from appearing on the same dais with Jack Benny to lecturing in Russia and Siberia.

An internationally acclaimed actor, his one-man shows, including the much heralded "The Shakespeare Man," which received a standing ovation at the Texas Shakespeare Festival, thrilled and entertained audiences throughout the U.S. and Great Britain.

Alfred lives with his wife, Irene, in Minnesota and spends his spare time with his three grown children and his grandson.

ABOUT THE ILLUSTRATOR

With a B.A. in fine arts from the University of Iowa and eight years experience as an instructor, William Arthur Luse III has spent the last twenty two years as a professional artist.

With over 30,000 patrons, he has created caricatures and portraits for everyone from barons of industry to "Joe six-pack."

Catch his act at the Renaissance Festival, corporate event, or. . .